21 Timeless Insights for Sales Success

An essential handbook that could

propel your selling career

Kurt Newman

First published 2013 by Sales Consultants Pty Ltd

Text © chapter authors, 2011
This design, format & edition © Sales Consultants Pty Ltd, 2013

ISBN: 978-0-646-90126-8 (paperback)

For general information on our products and services contact Sales Consultants Pty Ltd on 61 2 4861 4106 or visit our website www.salesconsultants.com.au or email info@salesconsultants.com.au.

What Others Have Said About This Book

The early to mid 20th century saw a boom in the creativity and spread of the sales professional remains a much maligned figure in casual conversation. However, the skills and motivation required to be successful in the field of sales has never been more important than in today's world. The rapid advances and changes in technology have had a large impact on the way buyers and sellers do business around the world, but the demand for and importance of sales skills has also never been greater.

In this book, Kurt distils the core attributes of what is required to be a top performing sales professional in today's market – and staying there. Whether the reader has been a sales person for 30 years or is just starting out, this book is an easy to read guide with practical advice based on experience and broad research over many years.

Terry Oomens
Director of Venues
Staging Connections

I have had the good fortune of working closely with Kurt Newman to reform large field sales forces across multiple industries, and it is no mistake that my success and the success of the sales teams was achieved following the teaching and coaching principles developed by Kurt. I believe sales is the greatest job in the world, a profession which touches almost everyone from a selling or buying perspective, and has opportunities and challenges which are utterly unique, and not addressed readily by tertiary education choices.

Over several years Kurt has developed and refined what I believe is the most effective and relevant relationship selling, coaching and performance improvement program available in any market, and I am proud to continue my learning and development with Kurt to the present day. The collection of articles which you are about to read are all designed to impart slices of the manifest knowledge that Kurt has developed on this subject, and will no doubt provide a number of aha moments for you, especially if you are currently in a sales role or managing sales people. I encourage you to allow these slices to challenge your thinking, and put them to the test knowing there have been many hundreds of successful sales people who have already done just that, and who will credit Kurt with being instrumental in helping them get to where they are today in the same way that I do.

Phil Saddleton
National Accounts Manager
Metcash Food & Grocery

In this book, Kurt demonstrates his incredible level of knowledge and experience in sales management, sales coaching and business development. His energy to be at the forefront of strategies to build sales capability is clearly evident. He personally continues to be an avid learner, always pushing the boundaries with his exploration of modern sales techniques and tools. He expertly combines this with traditional methods to create winning sales strategies that are aligned to the demand on a sales person in today's market place. With that in mind, Kurt demonstrates a true sense of empathy and practicality in this book — from his own experience he knows that it's not always plain sailing. In fact, selling is never "easy" and for many, today is particularly tough.

The content in this book addresses this and provides advice and techniques for those who are finding their selling life very challenging. Kurt provides insight through his in-depth knowledge of working through the sales cycle and his ability to organise and add structure to selling processes.

As a fellow consultant, striving to reach the status that Kurt has reached, a trusted adviser and value creation partner to his clients, I trust and value his professional insight and advice. I believe that this book and any form of engagement with Kurt Newman will truly add value to a salesperson at any level and enable better selling results.

Edward Turvil
Director – Business Transformation
Mercuri Urval

I have followed and practised Kurt Newman's sales strategies for over 20 years. His comments, beliefs and approach to mastering sales and creating long-term client relationships really do work; to the effect it has helped me greatly in establishing client relationships that have lasted well over 20 years. You too can master the art of sales and client relationships by following Kurt's proven practices.

Lyall Foy
Executive Manager – National Accounts
SKILLED Workforce Services

I would like to congratulate Kurt for what is an amazing read and one I have thoroughly enjoyed. We live in an ever-changing and evolving world, so I would highly recommend any sales professional read this e-book if they want to take the next step in enhancing their career.

Personal development in my mind is imperative in the success of any individual, and I feel this e-book goes a long way in creating those foundations…A must read!!!

Jim Haritonas
Regional Sales Manager
For Arts Sake

The book is clear and straightforward. It addresses sales as something everyone can practice, learn and enjoy – there really is a science to it. That said, it is clear that under new pressures many salespeople are guilty of overlooking the basics.

Sales today are more difficult in every way. Whether new to the industry or a 20-year veteran, there is something for all here. It's a simple read and I believe all sales people should refer back to it on a regular basis.

Mark Griffiths
Commercial Director
ACCO Australia Pty Ltd

I was first introduced to Kurt Newman from Sales Consultants four years ago while I was in the position of state sales manager. I had the privilege to be a part of the management training that was conducted by Kurt, which was tailored for our business and was a perfect fit. This book has grabbed my attention again as it felt like a positive review from a year ago. I regularly revisit articles to further my knowledge on sales. You will be quite surprised what this book can offer. It will open your eyes to sales styles, selling in tough times and the answer to gain more sales. I would be happy to speak to anyone who would like to find out more.

Brad Suffolk
Sales Manager, New South Wales
Inghams Enterprises Pty Limited

A comprehensive survival kit for both salespeople and leaders. Kurt addresses key sales obstacles that we face every day. The scene is set for 2013 and he quickly dispels the myth that selling is just a numbers game. The topics discussed are presented in a logical order, and as I read my way through them what sprung to mind was how a manager could expand on and workshop so much of this material with his or her people.

A recurring theme is the importance of attitude. If salespeople, and managers for that matter, are resilient, have strong desire, commitment and take ownership of their activity and results, then learning new stuff and using it are very achievable. If, on the other hand, their minds are in the wrong space, their beliefs don't support them when selling and they are prone to excuse making, then it will be an uphill battle.

As Kurt points out, more people try sales and fail than any other profession, yet the top salespeople will over-achieve whatever the market conditions.

Julian Griffith
Managing Director
The Good Peanut

It's great to find a concise book of common sense collected into such a readable form as this. Kurt Newman has produced a must-have read for anyone who is looking to understand the issues that lead to success and failure in selling. In a collection of short articles, Kurt deconstructs common fallacies and puts his finger on the essence of successful sales.

Thoroughly recommended.

Paul Beaumont
Managing Director
Full Throttle Consulting

A must read for anyone in a sales role! This book addresses all the elements involved in successful selling. It discusses techniques for sales personnel to develop awareness of personal impact and self-awareness, and provides a range of proven tools for increasing productivity and effectiveness in sales planning. If you want to develop a successful sales career, this book is essential reading.

Phil Meyer
Life Fellow
NZ Institute of Management

Acknowledgements

It's been a real pleasure getting to know so many salespeople and being part of their lives. They have shared their true inner selves during training and coaching sessions and expressed deep seated fears - but their desire and commitment to sales has propelled them on to great personal and professional victories. Many have achieved sales awards for outstanding performance. Many have now moved into sales coaching and/or sales management roles. Their experiences are what made this book possible and I got to know and understand more about myself as I got to know more about them.

There were many shared experiences including witnessing their very first sales confirmation, or breaking into an account they thought they would never have a hope of getting, or achieving a sales target that was thought out of reach. Some have attained great career milestones and in doing so they have set a standard of sales integrity that has lifted expectations of what is possible. Through their behaviour they have influenced and motivated others to become salespeople, who have in-turn, become better and more effective in their roles.

I appreciate the openness of the sales managers I have coached and mentored. Though they had completed a range of sales training and development programs with their employers, they wanted to continue to improve their sales competence. Their motivation was to become better sales coaches, and to do so they wanted to be able to demonstrate a higher standard of sales competence when working with their salespeople.

I want to thank the CEOs, business owners and general managers who allowed me into their companies and believed and trusted that we could achieve what needed to be achieved. Their honestly in expressing their goals, difficulties and frustrations was the foundation and the starting point of our relationship. The collaborative manner in which we worked together was a pleasure, though it wasn't always smooth sailing. At times difficult tasks and decisions had to be made from both perspectives, some of which caused me sleepless nights - but thank you for the experience and education.

Clients who pushed the bar higher and stretched everyone to a new reality of performance let me thank you. We all didn't necessarily enjoy the ride but are glad we did it.

To the difficult prospects who tried to give me a hard time, your behaviour helped me to remain grounded and use your rebuttal statements as examples for other salespeople to learn. To the prospects who expected the impossible turnaround let me wish you well.

To those of you who have written endorsements I thank you for taking the time to read the book and for your feedback. I appreciate the phone calls and emails and for letting me know it was like doing a mini refresher course.

And finally, and most importantly, thank you for selecting this book. I hope you gain the value that others have. If you have any questions or want to speak to me, please feel free to get in touch.

Kurt Newman, April 2013

Thank you to my wife and business partner June for your loving support and insight.

To Rebecca and Dominic Moore my daughter and son-in-law thank you for your commitment and attention to detail in editing this book.

Contents

About the Author

Kurt is the co-founder of Sales Consultants Pty Ltd. His expertise is in improving the sales effectiveness of his clients' businesses by generating more sales and in a more profitable manner. His clients range from small to multinational companies and he has successfully delivered projects in Australia, the Middle East and Asia.

As a salesperson, Kurt successfully sold products and services in the four major market/product segments; new product sales, consultative sales, relationship sales and retail. During his selling career he created record sales for three companies in two industries and won many sales awards for outstanding performance. This background gives him the advantage of being able to demonstrate selling competence, a powerful learning tool when coaching salespeople. He has guided many individual salespeople to greater success and many companies to vastly improved profits.

Kurt has studied business and human behaviour. His expertise and opinion is sought after on a range of sales related subjects in both print media (*Management Today, Training and Development and The Australian Financial Review*) and web-based business sites (*The BNET Report and Dynamic Business*). Furthermore, he has been featured in the Qantas In-Flight Radio Program 'Talking Business' and writes monthly articles for a global audience of subscribers.

Kurt is a Fellow of The Australian Institute of Management and a Licensed Associate of The Consulting Resource Group Canada.

Kurt can be contacted on:

Email – kurt@salesconsultants.com.au

LinkedIn – www.linkedin.com/pubkurt-newman/2/566/3a3

Facebook – www.facebook.com/Kurt.Newman166

Twitter – www.twitter.com/kurtnewman

Foreword

Salespeople are paid to get things done.

Of all the roles in today's organisations, none have the sustained pressure that salespeople work under – every day, every week, every quarter and every year.

The pressure to achieve, keep achieving and achieve more is relentless. Despite this pressure, many, many salespeople do achieve their targets; they get things done for their organisations – and satisfy customer demands in the process.

But – do they achieve as much as they could?

Most salespeople forget to do the one thing that will allow them to be successful in the daily pressured situations that are, for them, simply business as usual. In the words of the late Steven Covey, they forget – or often simply feel they don't have time – to "sharpen the saw". Covey was a master of human performance, who helped hundreds of thousands of people achieve more in their lives. His seventh habit of effectiveness was a reminder that we all – whether we're rocket scientists, brain surgeons, plumbers, accountants – or salespeople – need to take time to reflect on how we do what we do so we can do it better.

This short book will help every salesperson sharpen their saw.

If, as a professional salesperson you want to keep achieving – and achieve more – read this book. Along the way, you'll often nod your head in recognition of the simple truths that Kurt's pages contain.

Like any professional reviewing their practice, if this is the only benefit that you receive – then it's worth way more than the hour or two it will take to read. As a sales manager, editor and publisher, I've read hundreds of books on sales, marketing and human behaviour, and I guarantee that you'll get more from this book than just reminders. Every reader who looks closely into each short chapter will take away small gems which – over time – will convert into the thing we all need to deliver as salespeople – a healthy pipeline of sustainable sales.

Enjoy the read and look forward to achieving more.

Paul Sparks, Editor, Trend Business Publishing, Sydney, April, 20

1

How to use this book to develop the best sales habits

——————— Thinking and Action ———————

Over the past four years, I have written a series of blogs on the subject of professional selling and sales management.

The popularity of this series greatly exceeded my expectations, and, following feedback from readers, this book is based on the 20 most popular professional selling blogs. Each one has been extensively reviewed and updated, with the chapters written in a robust yet concise manner. The questions at the end of each chapter are designed to make what you have just read real for yourself and your world. The aim is to give you what you really need to know – and quickly.

What I'd like to suggest is to familiarise yourself with the book by skimming through it first. This will give you an overall sense of the content. You can then start at the beginning and work your way through each chapter or alternatively begin with those chapters that are most important to you. Whatever you decide to do is fine but please don't miss any chapters even if you think your know the content - treat yourself to some revision as this will keep it front of mind for when needed.

Only reading the book will give you information which is a good start but information in itself won't help you to create any shift in the sales skills you want to because reading is a passive way of learning. Therefore after reading each chapter take your time to complete the questions immediately following. This will provide you with the greatest opportunity to develop the competence you are aiming to achieve.

Each chapter is categorised and identified as either thinking or action, or a combination of both.

The thinking chapters relate to attitude. Your attitude is reflected in what you say, how you say it and non-verbally through your body language. A confident attitude is reflected in your behaviour. Clients generally like to deal with salespeople who have a positive and uplifting manner. Competent selling skills in itself is not enough to succeed.

The thinking chapters are designed to make you do just that - to think and reflect on what you are currently doing, what is working for you, and also what is not. It gives you the opportunity to learn what the best do and confirm what attitudes you have already internalised and isolates the ones you want to develop.

The action chapters are the things 'to do' and require you to implement the skills as highlighted. Select one skill at a time and focus on it until you feel comfortable that you can apply it under a range of selling conditions. This will also build you self-confidence of course. Then select another skill and go through the same process again. It may appear a slow way of developing selling skills but once you have mastered the skill it will be with you forever.

The examples given throughout each chapter include what you could say in a sales scenario and is there to make the learning easy to understand and apply.

As you read through each thinking or action or combination chapter, I would encourage you to reflect on what you have learnt then apply it, then learn some more, reflect on it and apply once again. By repeating this cycle it gives you the opportunity to self-correct during the reflection period and apply the corrected variation – and this is how you can fine tune any attitude or skill for that matter. Successful salespeople develop their sales competence in this manner. The book's aim, as much as possible and practicable, is to provide you with answers to the 'what', 'how' and 'why' questions in an attempt to give you complete yet succinct understanding.

Keep this book in your car or wherever it will be visible and easily accessible so it can be referred to as often as you need. As a suggestion, after you have completed the book in its entirety familiarise yourself with the content every 6 months by rereading it - the refresher will keep you sharp.

You are welcome to contact me if you have any questions or would like to let me know how you are progressing.

Let me wish you great sales success.

2

Six things you must do to create sales this year

If forecasters are correct with their predictions…

_____ Action _____

This year will be a challenging year, particularly if the economies of countries such as China and India slow down. But whatever happens, we still need to sell and do better than we did in the previous year. Interestingly though, 15% of salespeople will overachieve their sales targets irrespective of what the economy does.

So what do consistently high performing salespeople do? They influence the behaviour of their clients, who react to economic conditions and change their behaviour. High-calibre salespeople know this and they adapt how they sell and the sales strategies they use to maximise their sales opportunities.

In challenging economic times, clients tend to be slow in decision making, focus on price and want to minimise their responsibility as we explain below.

Slow in making a decision

The higher the sales value, the greater the stall in making decisions. The fear of making a wrong decision immobilises the client so they procrastinate and no decision is made. Alternatively, they invite others into the decision making process, therefore avoiding taking responsibility for making a decision whilst extending the buying cycle.

Price focused

A price focus is to get the lowest possible cost and can include one or more of the following actions:

• The client invites multiple suppliers to quote on their product or service needs. In some cases, reverse online bidding is introduced which can rapidly drive prices down

• Long term suppliers' cost prices are checked with their competitors to ensure the client is getting the best price. This has become common practice

• Client tactics are used to undermine the value of a supplier's product or service. For example, to affect the salesperson's self-worth, the product or service isn't named but referred to as a commodity.

Minimise responsibility

Clients are expecting suppliers to take a greater share of responsibility through extended warranties and payment terms, shorter ROI time frames, reduced installation times and other guarantees. Clients appear to feel comfortable with these behaviours, so you can expect to experience one or more of these tactics in the coming year.

So what can we do to influence a client's behaviour?

1) Ask the right questions

Salespeople ask questions but tend not to drill down into enough specifics due to a fear of intruding. Identifying a problem in itself won't necessarily motivate a client to act. But if the effect of a problem is uncovered, your chances are multiplied considerably. For example, *"What are the core challenges in growing sales in your division?"* This could be followed by, *"What effect has this had on your profitability?"* or *"How has this impacted on you personally?"* The client will not only be mentally engaged but also emotionally involved.

2) Actively grow client relationships

Build on the credibility and trust you have established, particularly with your long-term clients. Too often long-term clients are taken for granted. If they feel they are taken for granted, they are. This can lead to their looking for another supplier. With every client visit learn more about them on a personal and business level. Regularly reinforce your personal commitment to them by, for example, sending them interesting newspaper or magazine articles. It will show that you care and are thinking of them.

3) Differentiate yourself

For differentiation to be effective it must be of value to the client and something that truly separates you from your competitors. Done well, your differentiator will lock out your competitors. What one client values may be different from what another values, so the differentiation needs to be tailored. Begin by showing that you are not focused on pushing your product or service. Instead ask questions to show the client that you are personally interested and are seeking a deeper level of understanding of their situation.

Why not ask clients, with whom you have had a solid business relationship, why they prefer to deal with you rather than your competitors? To get a balanced opinion also ask if there are any areas you could improve. Don't become defensive if you are given some criticism. Instead, thank them for being so candid. This process could feel uncomfortable and even risky at first, but the feedback is vital information needed to develop your differentiation strategy.

4) Reach out for new business

Regularly set time aside to prospect for new business. This can include attending networking functions, sending emails, researching on Google or LinkedIn, making phone calls or drop-in visits, and sending correspondence by standard mail. Work on two or three prospecting activities that work for you. You may not necessarily succeed with one or two attempts to get an appointment but persist and you will succeed.

If you don't regularly pursue new business opportunities and just rely on existing clients to generate your sales revenue, then sales will shrink over time.

5) Ask for referrals

There are only two types of referrals – cold or hot. Unfortunately, too many salespeople work with cold referrals and are not aware of it. A cold referral is one where the prospect doesn't know you and is not expecting your call.

A cold referral is created when you are given a name and phone number of a prospect, and that is the only information you have. A hot referral is one where the prospect knows who you are and is expecting your call. You also have background information about the prospect's situation and you know something about them personally. Converting a cold referral into a hot one is simply a matter of asking more questions. For example, *"Why do you think Jenny would be interested?"* or *"Who is their current supplier?"* Ask your client to call the prospect and let them know you will be contacting them. The prospect will then be expecting your call. Hot referrals result in more qualified prospects which reduce the selling cycle time significantly.

6) Continue your professional sales development

Elite sportspeople use coaches because they want to fine tune their skills, learn any new developments in their field and improve themselves. High performing salespeople share this same perspective and invest time, effort and money into their ongoing development. This can be by attending courses, hiring a sales coach, attending seminars, and reading sales and business books and articles.

The year ahead will provide sales growth opportunities for high calibre salespeople no matter what the economy does. So why shouldn't you be one of them?

What Does This Chapter Mean in Your World?

1. What is your prediction for sales in the foreseeable future?

....

....

....

....

2. Why do you think the outlook is the way you describe it?

....

....

....

....

3. How do most of your clients behave when business conditions are tough?

....

....

....

....

4. In the past what was your reaction when clients behaved in this way?

....

....

....

....

5. Based on what you have learnt what changes will you now implement?

....

....

....

....

6. What will you do to maximise your sales despite any economic prediction?

....

....

....

....

3

The five common myths in sales and what really works

Sales myths are harmless in themselves.
After all they are only myths right?

_____ Thinking _____

No, wrong. Salespeople and sales managers who believe these myths and act on them unwittingly create client relationship problems and lose sales.

Myth 1 – It's a numbers game

Having a list of names and repeatedly "cold calling" until the prospective client finally speaks to you is impersonal and is both tedious for the salesperson and can project a product peddling image. The prospective client in many cases will reject you by becoming defensive or aggressive and may even hang up the phone. So how do you develop a trusting relationship when the prospective client is just another number? The answer is you can't.

What works?

Focus on the quality of each interaction and not purely on a number. Base your sales calls on prospective clients who have genuine potential to buy your product or service. By researching and finding common industry or business problems relating to the prospective client that your product or service can solve will make the phone call so much easier. This is because you will be able to gain involvement around an issue they are interested in discussing. For example *"....Do you mind if I ask what do you do when your current supplier is out of stock?... We have worked with numerous companies that have experienced the same difficulty and through our extensive network can guarantee with a 98.5% accuracy that your order will be delivered in full within 24 hours...Is this something you would like to discuss in more detail over a meeting?..."*

When calling, establish an open and friendly manner aimed at creating mutual respect. Use open-ended questions, survival phrases and good language. Begin by getting yourself in the right mental frame of mind by deleting language that will disengage them. For example, do not use or even think in terms such as *"cold calling."* Replace this with *"new calls"* because that describes what it is – a new call. There is nothing *"cold"* about calling someone for the first time.

Myth 2 – For every "no" you are closer to a "yes"

Using the same approach for every call and expecting a different outcome just doesn't make sense. The chance of a *"no"* becoming a *"yes"* is highly unlikely. If it did, it would be more through pure luck than anything else. A high volume of calls in itself won't produce sales success.

What works?

Learn what has been going wrong with your sales calls and change what needs to be changed in any area of your approach. This could, for example, be how you project yourself over the phone and affect things like your vocal tone. Do you sound confident or is there a slight quiver in your voice? What about the pace you are speaking? Is it too fast and the prospective client needs to ask you to repeat what you have said? Is your pace too slow? In this case they may hang up or tell you to hurry it along? Also be aware of the phrases you use. Too often unconsciously negative phrases are used that automatically create rebuttals. Read the following out aloud and hear the difference between *"What you will* have to do is…" and "What we will need to do is…" Which statement would you respond to more positively?

If you are getting too many no's perhaps you may need to also review your selling skills?

Myth 3 – You don't need a script

Yes you do. Not using a script creates its own set of problems. For example, if you were to mentally freeze half way through a sentence and with no notes to refer to, you could find yourself verbally fumbling using non-words such as "Umm", "Err", or "Okay" and therefore sound unprofessional. If the experience is traumatic enough this could directly lead to sales call reluctance.

What works?

Depending on whether you are trying to get an appointment or selling over the phone, your approach and the amount of time you spend on the phone will vary. Develop your script and list core questions you will ask. Then practice, practice, and practice until it feels comfortable and comes naturally to you. Your script is there only as a back-up should you get stuck and is not to be read verbatim as listening to someone reading from a script is impersonal and disengages the prospective client. Knowing your script to the point of sounding natural and this will also build your self-confidence, which will also in turn be reflected in your vocal tone.

Myth 4 – You need to welcome rejection because it is part of sales

By expecting rejection there is a good chance it will happen. No one likes to be rejected. But you can attract rejection if you sound nervous and anxious when you approach a prospective client. Rejection can also happen when a prospective client is simply having a bad day and you happen to call.

What works?

Prepare for the possibility of being rejected by developing skills to turn around any rebuttal or sales objection (See Chapter 17). What is really important to understand is that any rejection is a business refusal and therefore not to be taken as personal rejection. You might be proposing, for example, an appointment that has been refused. This doesn't mean you are rejected; it could simply be a timing issue. What is worth remembering is a prospective client may reject an appointment this time but may agree the next time you call.

Myth 5 – Close often and close hard

This is high pressure selling and it's from the old school of sales. It is a single-minded focus to try to sell a product or service with minimal regard for the client's real needs or how they may feel. The response is often a sales objection. If pushed too hard they will hang up the phone, or if it's a walk-in sales call they will ask you to leave. This does not build long term trusting business relationships.

What works?

Don't assume the prospective client will buy what you think they should buy. It will only attract sales objections. Relax and live in the moment with the prospective client by asking a range of questions - preferably open and qualifying questions to uncover what they really need. For example, *"What will the restructure mean to you in terms of your career"…"Under the new structure who will be making the purchasing decisions?"* Then actively listen to their response. Your aim in the first instance is to create trust and not to get the sale. Yes you read correctly – not to get the sale. When you create trust and build a solid relationship, the prospective client will be in an open frame of mind to listen to what product or service you are recommending and why. Closing will feel a natural conclusion to the sales interview for both yourself and the prospective client. When closing in this manner it is not uncommon for the prospective client to initiate the close and therefore they will feel they have bought from you rather than having been sold to.

There are many other sales myths, some of which have been around for decades, but the ones listed are the most common. Myths need to be acknowledged for what they are. A myth that was perpetuated by someone a long time ago, and for reasons unknown, perhaps remain to this day due to simple ignorance. Never act on a myth but always implement what really does work.

What Does This Chapter Mean in Your World?

1. What myths other than those listed have you heard?

....

....

....

....

2. Have you acted on a myth? If so, what was the outcome?

....

....

....

3. What did you learn from the experience?

....

....

....

4. What have you learnt about sales myths?

....

....

....

....

4

Attitude in sales – so what's the big deal?

What would you think is most important in sales: knowledge, skills or attitude?

_____ Thinking _____

Let's begin with the difference between knowledge and skills:

- Knowledge is gained through education, facts and information

- A skill is the ability to apply knowledge that has been acquired through training or experience

Why is it that salespeople, who have in some cases many years of industry and product knowledge coupled with a good standard of selling skills, fail to achieve their potential? Is the missing link attitude and, if so, is it really that integral to sales success? The answer is yes.

Attitude

Your attitude is formed by your experiences and what you have seen and believe. This can be either positive or negative and impact on how you react or respond to anything from other people, objects, and activities through to your work environment and your personal life.

Three elements that form your attitude are:

1. Thoughts – this is what you think about, and your beliefs on, a subject. This conscious part directs your logic, rational thinking, choices and decisions[1]

2. Feelings – this is how you feel; your emotions about a topic. Your emotions are so powerful that they often overrule your knowledge[2]

3. Actions – your actions reflect your attitudes, which in turn affect how you behave. This can be conscious, or deep seated and unconscious. Actions are often driven by dissatisfaction with the status quo.

Each of the three elements will influence overall attitude and sometimes, but not always, one is affected differently by the other elements. For example, you may think and feel you don't have the ability to perform a particular sales role but will act as if you can because you want the income the sales position may offer.

Change in Attitude

Attitude can dominate behaviour - but it is possible to change or modify it, when the desired motivation for change is the driving force. For example, if a salesperson is consumed with passion to become the best salesperson in the company they will commit to going through the discomfort of behaviour change and learn the required sales skills in order to achieve their goal.

Change in attitude can be:

• *Attitude change through observation*

An example would be you notice and admire how your sales manager handled a difficult selling situation. At that moment in time you decide you want to develop the same behaviour and skill level so you ask your sales manager if they would coach and mentor you

---

1, 2 Ron Willingham, 2006, *The Inner Game of Selling*, Free Press

- *Attitude change through persuasion*

Through discussions you may now truly understand and see the logic and feel the strong emotional attraction that having a different attitude can provide. This could be closer relationships with family and co-workers resulting in your becoming more patient; or taking greater responsibility

- *Attitude change through conflict*

No one likes to feel conflict but it can be a powerful motivator for change. It happens when the internal tension of conflicting beliefs builds to the point of being so strong this often creates very uncomfortable thoughts and feelings that something has to give. To reduce the internal escalating pressure you decide to change your attitude.

Attitude check

Let's face it, selling isn't for the faint hearted and there can be times when getting sales can be tough. With mounting pressure from various sources, one of the first things that can be tested is your attitude.

To check your attitude, answer the following questions…honestly.

1. I currently think and feel negative? *Yes/No*

2. I see my current problems as weighing me down? *Yes/No*

3. I overeat and or drink too much alcohol or take drugs? *Yes/No*

4. I stopped going to the gym or stopped my exercise program? *Yes/No*

5. I don't have someone to confide in, such as a family member, colleague or mentor/coach? *Yes/No*

6. I don't have written goals. *Yes/No*

If you score 3 or more *'yes'* responses then you need to take action to realign your attitude and maximise your potential.

Knowledge, skills and attitude are the three most important attributes for your success. Product knowledge and skills can be acquired from the first day you start a new sales job, and will continue throughout your time with the company. Let me ask you, what if a salesperson you work with has an impressive level of industry and product knowledge and they are competent at selling but lack the right attitude? They complain about every problem that arises and that everything is too much to bother with. How do you work with this type of person? How do you feel when you are around this person? The answer to the first question is *"with great difficulty"*. The answer to the second question is *"uninspired, bored"* or perhaps even *"angry?"* You would want to avoid communicating with them, and even stay clear of them.

In my opinion, if a salesperson refuses to develop the attitudes that complement their role in sales, then they should look for another career. They are just not suitable for a sales role.

What Does This Chapter Mean in Your World?

1. What are the 3 most important factors in sales?

....

....

....

....

2. Why is having product and industry knowledge not enough?

....

....

....

3. What are the 3 elements that form our attitude?

....

....

....

....

4. What are the 3 influences that can change attitude?

....

....

....

....

5. Provide an example when you changed your attitude. What were the circumstances?

....

....

....

....

6. What areas of attitude would you like to improve?

....

....

....

....

5

What makes an 'A' player in sales?

I asked friends who are not in sales
what they think of salespeople

—————————— Thinking ——————————

Typical responses included *"They talk too much"*, *"They are pushy"* and *"They can't be trusted."* They rate salespeople in the same or similar way as they would politicians in terms of lacking in trust and credibility. If you were to ask people at random, you would more than likely get similar answers. So why does the sales profession get such a bad rap?

The truth is stranger than fiction because those who are successful in sales actually don't fit this negative sales stereotype. In fact, these salespeople often have behaviours opposite of what many people would think or expect.

What is interesting about sales is that more people try sales and fail than any other profession. This is because the entry level is usually low and most people assume it requires little in the way of intelligence or ability. Those who have tried sales and failed discovered it's a tough career and one not for those who are timid. Most lack the desire and commitment needed to succeed in sales. This is particularly true for those who work in the corporate sector and 'do sales' for a year or two because it will help them progress their careers. They soon learn that sales is different and many happily go back to their previous roles.

What makes sales different from other careers is:

- Every day you need to handle rejection and even hostility at times

- You have little or no control of the behaviour of prospects or clients

- You are measured in every way — from the number of sales calls you do through to conversion rates and profit margins

- You need to adapt quickly to many different personality types

- A positive outlook is needed, particularly when faced with client related problems

- You need self-control. This is the ability to balance the pressure of needing to achieve sales targets and grow client relationships.

So what are the common traits of the most successful salespeople? What makes them stand out? Based on our research and experience, gained in 25 years of developing sales competence in salespeople, the following attributes appear in the make-up of the most successful:

1. Desire

Desire is the passion, the drive to succeed, and the inner fire that fuels and propels them into action. Desire comes from being dissatisfied with the current situation. The greater the dissatisfaction the greater the desire being ignited from within.

2. Commitment

Commitment is being welded to an idea, outcome, or an action. It's the *"stick-ability"* to overcome obstacles whilst moving forward toward their goal. These obstacles can be work related, such as competitor challenges or personal self-doubt.

3. Independence

These salespeople are attracted to the freedom that sales offers — the sense of feeling self-employed. They like to be self-sufficient and maintain full control over their activities, such as who to contact and when. Along with independence comes a dislike of rules and regulations which they tend to *"bend"* when given a chance. They tend to upset individuals in the support team because of their unrealistic expectations at times. They expect loyalty and full support from their company so they can do what they do best – sell.

They avoid paperwork, report writing and what they consider red tape. Reports, when written, are brief and to the point. These successful salespeople like people. They enjoy being with them and delight in influencing but seldom care deeply whether others like them. This enables them not to fall prey for the need for approval or to be timid.

4. Trustworthy

Trust is central to building client relationships. Trust is developed when integrity and competence are demonstrated with every interaction. The client has a firm belief in the salesperson's reliability, their predictable behaviour and honesty. It is not uncommon for the client to proceed with a decision even though they may not fully understand how the solution will work because of the level of trust that has been established. They don't need proof to make their decision and competitors are automatically locked out.

5. Productivity

These top sales performers have a need to generate more sales. They are energetic, enthusiastic and want to see tangible results for their effort. This energy may not always be shown openly. Trade shows and conferences are seen as a working holiday. They socialise with a purpose by connecting with individuals with whom they have something in common, whether it's business or some other personal pursuit that may result in a sale.

6. Traditional

Contrary to what the average person may think about salespeople being impulsive and somewhat undisciplined, in reality these salespeople like routine and hate having it interrupted, for example if they have to attend a meeting that wasn't planned. They embrace structure and order. They don't try unproven ideas simply because they are new and different. Radical ideas are rejected outright. They stick with what they know has been tried and works even if it is dated. However, once convinced about a fresh approach or idea, they will do whatever it takes to develop the new skill or behaviour.

7. Non Academic

This doesn't mean salespeople are not intelligent. Their practical nature leans toward doing rather than studying something they may never use. Theory without a practical application is rejected outright. They would prefer to spend time developing skills that will result in more sales and earn them income. These salespeople are natural doers rather than reflective thinkers. This doesn't mean they don't evaluate what may have gone wrong during the sales call. They quickly evaluate what went wrong and why, and then focus on what they will do during the next sales call to correct or fine tune their skills. They don't waste time agonising about things.

8. Opportunistic

Salespeople of this calibre are calm and relaxed, yet have a high level of energy and thrive on challenges. They have more physical energy than most and they look for a way to get a positive outcome in every sales activity. Satisfaction is derived from overcoming difficulties. They capitalise on opportunities by beating the system to win sales which can sometimes upset management and the internal support team.

9. Able to Handle Fear

Successful salespeople are known for their ability to cope with pressure, handle criticism, rejection or anger. They know a sale requires a level of assertiveness that must occur naturally without fear or timidity, all whilst being able to empathise with the client's situation. They have learnt not to take rejection or conflict as a personal affront. Salespeople who take rejection personally or have difficulty with conflict will become overly cautious, timid and avoid prospecting, and therefore lose sales opportunities.

10. Don't Need Approval

These salespeople are naturally social individuals, and whilst appearing friendly they are focused on achieving their sales objectives. They don't need to be liked or seek approval from others. They are not concerned with what a prospective client may think of them personally. Instead, they earn professional respect which empowers them to ask the tough questions in order to uncover problems that other salespeople miss and this ultimately leads to them winning the business.

11. Status Seeking

The best salespeople seek recognition as proof of their ability and importance. They want to be seen as experts on what is right and in the best interest for their clients. They regard themselves as well intentioned people who are willing to help others. This may explain why many are involved in community based organisations in their spare time. They enjoy the power, authority and status that is achieved through their hard work, and are strongly aware of image and reputation. They are comfortable in rewarding themselves for their successes, which explains why many drive prestige cars and wear quality clothing.

What Does This Chapter Mean in Your World?

1. In your opinion why do you think more people try sales and fail?

....

....

....

....

2. Why is sales different from other careers?

....

....

....

....

3. What is the difference between desire and commitment?

....

....

....

....

4. What is meant by the term non-academic?

....

....

....

....

5. What have you done to handle criticism and rejection in sales?

....

....

....

....

6. What attributes are you going to develop to become the salesperson you want to be?

....

....

....

....

6

Selling in tough times

Fewer than 50% of today's business-to-business salespeople have ever sold during an economic downturn

_____ Thinking and Action _____

If you were in sales in the previous economic downturns of 1980, 1990 or 2001, you will remember what it was like - not a pleasant experience. However economic downturns can provide great opportunities for those who don't follow the herd. Many companies batten down their hatches and are totally consumed with cost reductions to the point of preventing their company from performing the way it is meant to. For example, one business owner I spoke to during the 2001 downturn spoke proudly of how he was *"controlling costs"* by collecting every employee's pen and pencil at the end of a working day and redistributing these first thing the next morning. When an employee's pen was out of ink they had to ask him for a replacement. As ludicrous as this may read to you, sadly it's the truth.

The batten down the hatches type managers hope that when they open their hatches the economic downturn has moved on. When the economy returns to growth, which it always invariably does, their company is often in such a weak position that they are unable to take advantage of the upswing. This leaves them as easy prey to a competitor takeover or they may simply go out of business because a stronger competitor now dominates their market.

The fact is that the selling environment during tough times changes and we need to adapt in order to survive and grow.

Before we look at what we can do let's look at the past to learn what happened in previous economic downturns:

1. Clients, and particularly prospective clients, became more risk averse and preferred to deal with suppliers who they knew, trusted and had a good track record with. This can make it challenging, but not impossible, to win their business.

2. Trying to secure an appointment with the decision-maker was difficult and almost impossible, particularly with medium to large organisations that implemented complex buying procedures. Selling cycles had become longer because more people got involved in the decision process with some personnel being moved to different geographical locations.

3. The new protocol meant a dramatic increase in the volume of sales calls, proposals, demonstrations, and presentations. Sales pipelines became full of questionable opportunities that resulted in minimal, if any, impact on sales. Salespeople concerned about their lack of prospect numbers in the sales pipeline didn't qualify as effectively as they once did resulting in "rubbery" opportunities. Sales forecasts became unrealistic, and in time some salespeople and sales managers lost their jobs. Clients became more cautious and, unless the salesperson could clearly demonstrate greater value than their competitors, no decision was made.

4. Some salespeople resorted to high pressure selling tactics to push their clients into buying. This type of behaviour shows a salesperson with limited selling ability and a lack of respect for the other person while creating the risk of damaging the relationship permanently. If a sale was made, there was always a strong risk the order would be cancelled as soon as the salesperson left their premises.

5. Discounting. This may appear as an easy fix to a short-term problem - however discounting creates other problems. The most obvious is a greater

volume of products or services needing to be sold in order to generate the same amount of profit. If the increase in sales volume isn't achieved, the company will be in a weaker financial position. Discounting also negatively impacts on an industry and is too great a price to pay because it creates a precedent that cannot be easily reversed.

6. Making more cold calls. Simply increasing sales activity levels without a sound sales strategy won't necessarily produce more sales - it only increases costs and frustrates the salesperson. In an economic downturn, prospective clients are reluctant to change suppliers unless the competing supplier can offer additional value the current supplier can't or won't. For example, these could be an extended warranty, additional product features at no extra cost, or generous trading terms.

So how can you take advantage of an economic downturn?

1. Think growth

Salespeople who are only in survival mode tend to overreact to problems and their decisions are often fear-based. In this state of mind they are also risk aversive and have a narrow, tunnel perspective. To begin, think growth and set clearly defined written goals for the next 30 days. Then identify the action steps you need on a daily and weekly basis to make it happen. By focusing on your goals and activities you will minimise the chance of being distracted.

2. Re-evaluate who you associate with

You cannot afford, nor would you want to be affected by, people who are constantly looking for and speaking gloom. You know the type of person I am referring to. When you ask them *"how are you?"* they respond in a flat monotone *"Not bad"* or *"Things could be better"* and you hear the silent sigh. Their body language mirrors their words - stooped shoulders, weak hand shake, and little or no eye contact. It becomes a self-fulfilling prophecy, also known as the law of psychological reciprocity, that what you think of most of the time will actually happen. Associate with people who are already successful, or well on their way, and develop networks that have a positive, uplifting impact on you.

3. Build a brick wall around key clients

This means to develop personal and business relationships that cannot be easily duplicated by your competitors. Focus on your best-selling opportunities to drive sales growth through the value you provide for your clients. Get to know their business intimately, who their competitors are, and the issues they face. Introduce your client to others who could help them. For example, the top salesperson, let's call him John, of a company operating in the fine paper industry had one of his clients share a major problem with him. He had won a large printing order with a tight deadline and his foreman was off with the flu and expected to be away for some time. John had a mate who was a printer and asked if he would do the job over the weekend at John's client's premises. He did this and the job was delivered on time. This is a true story – and to John's unexpected delight, his client who used to give him 60% of his paper needs business gave it all to him as a token of appreciation. Ask yourself why would John's client give any of his business to a competitor when he has a supplier who personally cares about him and his business?

To identify your best selling opportunities rank your clients in terms of sales revenue starting from the highest to the lowest – the top 1-20 Category A; 21-75 Category B; and 76-100 Category C. You will now know where to allocate most of your time.

Thoroughly qualify every sales opportunity so your sales pipeline is full of genuine business potential. You don't want to waste your time on anything else. It's not having a big number of opportunities in your pipeline that counts but the quality and your conversion ratio to confirmed sales really does.

4. Focus on selling value

Value could be reliability, security, stability, safety, guarantees or warranties, and peace of mind. Value is personal — what works for one may not for another, so you will need to adapt your value proposal to individual clients. Also think in terms of tangible and intangible value - tangible value relates to a measurable outcome such as cost saving or increased revenue whereas intangible value is harder to measure and can be subjective. An example of an intangible value would be the trust a client feels for you.

Selling in tough times requires adapting to the new realities but can provide many opportunities. Looking at the past can be a guide for appropriate action during such time. Don't follow the herd, take calculated risks, remain innovative, and stay close to your clients both on a business as well as a personal basis. In the end you will make more sales, enjoy yourself more, and be in a stronger position when the economy swings back to an upward curve.

What Does This Chapter Mean in Your World?

1. If you were in sales during any of the previous economic downturns what are 3 things you remember about it?

....

....

....

2. What was the greatest challenge you faced in trying to achieve sales revenue during this period?

....

....

....

3. What are you going to do to ensure you only have qualified prospects in your sales pipeline?

....

....

....

4. What can you do to protect yourself from chronic negative people without offending them?

....

....

....

....

5. What intangible value do you think you currently or plan to give your clients?

....

....

....

....

6. What will you do differently when the next major economic downturn arrives?

....

....

....

....

7

Selling professional services in a down economy

Despite the current economic conditions, 15% of salespeople will overachieve, 25% will leave the selling profession, and a staggering 60% will struggle

_____ Thinking and Action _____

What causes such devastation to the sales profession? In our experience, the two most prominent reasons are indeed a change in client behaviour and a salesperson's inability to adapt.

Client behaviour

Client behaviour changes when the economy slows down, or in some cases a perception of an impending slowdown, and the longer the duration of the slowdown, the more intense the behaviour. Put simply it's because clients are under pressure to save money and to maximise the service received for every dollar spent. Unfortunately, this too often means they go for the cheapest option.

Clients also become risk averse and will prefer to deal with people they know, trust and have had dealings with, even if those relationships had their problems.

You could experience all or most of the following in client behaviour changes:

• The number of people involved in the client decision process may increase, making the sales environment more complex and extending the selling cycle

• The decision to buy your products or services may now be controlled by more senior management. This is particularly true for large organisations that are experiencing difficult trading conditions. Decentralisation is replaced by centralisation for greater cost control. In some cases, and depending on the amount of money involved, the decision can be pushed to a regional level or transferred to another country that heads the region

• The client needs to justify the purchase and may ask for a return on investment in a reduced time frame

• The budget for your products or services may have been approved by the client some time ago but funding may have to go through the approval process again, possibly involving a new submission of proposals

• The client may ask for a change in trading terms. This could be to extend the payment period

• A client who would normally have called to give you more business may now have to ask for cost details and be required to get multiple quotations. If this should happen to you, don't take it personally. The client is probably under a lot of pressure from senior management.

So what is it that high sales performers do that makes them prosper in a down economy? They focus on being positive, grow sales, work smarter, and remain strategic.

Being Positive

By consistently thinking and behaving in a positive manner, they know the client will feel uplifted in their presence. With the amount of negativity during an economic downturn it's a pleasant experience for clients to deal with a salesperson who has a positive disposition. For example, when they greet a client they use an uplifting vocal tone. High performers protect themselves from habitual negative people by minimising their contact with them. They go so far as to avoid them. They regularly re-evaluate who they associate with and are conscious of their own thoughts. They develop networks with people who have similar attributes.

Sales Growth

They always think in terms of sales growth. Having a volume of sales calls for both existing and prospective clients is their starting point. Proposals are written to achieve a measurable outcome for the client and not a product or service push. When in a face-to-face selling situation they don't sell traditional features and benefits but concentrate on selling value, reliability, security and/or peace of mind. Over time these qualities build an emotional sense of ease for the client, loyalty and solid relationships.

Working Smart

They concentrate most of their selling time and effort on key clients, the category 'A' top 20%. This is because they know these clients have the greatest potential to produce the revenue they need to achieve their sales target. It's easier to increase sales with a client who is giving you 70% of their business to 80% than it is from a client business 5% to 15%. The number of face-to-face meetings with category 'B' clients is reduced and substituted, at least in part with emails or phone calls. The category 'C' clients are delegated to client service personnel to manage. This is because the sales revenue doesn't justify the cost of a face-to-face sales call. They qualify every sales opportunity thoroughly which results in time being saved and their sales pipeline has sales revenue potential that makes forecasting more accurate.

With many competitors cutting back on service levels to save money during an economic downturn, high performing salespeople target prospective clients who are not being serviced or are serviced poorly by their competitors. They do their homework and develop a detailed client profile. They learn about each prospective client's industry, market positioning, number of employees, other divisions and corporate challenges. They study the annual report if it is a public company. They actively participate and search for background information on social media websites such as LinkedIn, Facebook and Google

Plus. Some salespeople have additional personal contact with their key clients via Facebook.

Strategic Positioning

The weakest client relationship is one where the client sees every supplier as the same, with the only differentiator being price. High performing salespeople don't waste their time with these price hypersensitive people. They know the games these clients play such as making a sales enquiry that appears genuine but in reality is a price check of a favoured supplier's quotation. A long-term, mutually beneficial relationship is not possible under these conditions. Margins become too slim, the client tends to be overly demanding, and payment of invoices is slow.

What high performing salespeople do is they position themselves as the trusted advisor for their clients; an expert the client feels comfortable with to openly discuss any matter and know it will be kept in confidence. They develop a close personal and business relationship that locks out competitors. In a desperate attempt to win business, competitors will reduce their price by heavily discounting. This won't work in many instances because the client receives far greater value than just price – peace of mind. The salesperson is held in such high regard that the client will ask for the salesperson's opinion on products and services unrelated to what the salesperson is selling.

Selling in a down economy is tough. With most competitors believing it's all about lowering prices to win business it provides opportunities that are not present during other economic cycles. If a client perceives all suppliers within a market segment as being the same, they will go for the lowest cost. High performers know this and provide value way beyond the product or service itself, which then becomes the differentiator for the client and the reason why they give them their business. The fact that 15% of salespeople overachieve in a down economy validates this.

What Does This Chapter Mean in Your World?

1. In your opinion why do you think 15% of salespeople overachieve despite an economic downturn?

....

....

....

....

2. From your experience how do clients behave differently in a slow economy?

....

....

....

....

3. Why do clients become risk aversive?

....

....

....

4. What can you do to become consistently positive?

....

....

....

....

5. What strategies can you put into place so the client doesn't see your product or service as a commodity?

....

....

....

....

6. What are you going to do to continue sales growth no matter what the economy does?

....

....

....

....

8

How to overcome negative thinking in sales

*How many of us can go for an hour or a day
without having a negative thought?*

_____ Thinking _____

If you are completely honest with yourself, the answer would be you couldn't or with great difficulty.

Have you ever benefited from a negative thought? Has it helped you achieve great sales results or a happy personal life? Has it made you feel exhilarated or made you feel good about yourself? If not, why do we have negative thoughts and persist with them?

Unfortunately, the great majority of people think and speak negatively without realising it. Perhaps it's social conditioning to the point that we have become unconscious to the amount of negativity we are being bombarded with, particularly from media sources such as television, print media and radio. Have we become so desensitised that we think negativity is a normal state of being?

Unfortunately negative thinking can become a habit, creating a flow-on effect of other problems. Depending on the individual, these problems usually manifest themselves in low levels of physical, mental, and emotional energy. Many experience an inability to complete tasks and therefore achieve their sales targets. They use excuses and blame others for their lack of achieving their sales numbers. Left unchecked, in time these salespeople can suffer from low self-worth. For example, low self-worth individuals tend to have:[3]

- More emotional problems

- Attain lower earnings

- Take criticism defensively

- Are more resistant to change

- Expect to be rejected

- Suffer more stress related illness

What we need to be mindful of is that we attract what we think of most of the time – this is the law of attraction. This law has no judging capacity, so it doesn't differentiate between positive or negative, wanted or unwanted, or whether you believe it or not. Think of the things you want to happen and not the things you don't want to happen, otherwise what you are trying to avoid will become the dominant thought and the law of attraction will kick in. For example, if you used the phrase *"I need more sales"* repeatedly over and over the result will be *"need more sales."* This negative thought will prevent any change in sales from happening. To change, think in terms of *"I am taking positive action now to build on the sales volume I already have."* The key is to focus on what you have and not on what you don't have. You will also feel better because you are giving yourself credit for what is being done well so far in order to achieve your goal.

In the short term, a positive affirmation statement you make will clash with your belief system. Your belief system determines how you think, feel and behave. If you are already a competent salesperson and want to change your sales results, you need to eradicate the beliefs that create negative results. A belief is a statement that has been supported by repeatedly thinking and feeling

---

3   Everett T Robinson MA and Ken Keis MBA, 2011, **Self-Worth Inventory** CRG Consulting Resource Group International Inc

that a current situation, whether real or imagined, is true.

Beliefs can feel compelling, irrational, emotionally charged, lacking in facts, and not based on personal experience.

Where can you begin?

Write down and repeat the positive affirmation whenever you get the opportunity until you create a new belief system. For example, on two successive occasions you missed out on getting the sale confirmed with a particular client. You may have told yourself that you probably won't get the next one. Stop! Replace the negative thoughts and feelings before they become locked in your belief system. Look at the facts that make this sales call different from the previous ones. This could be the lessons you learnt about the client's manner of negation, the type of questions you need to ask and that you are completely prepared for any situation that may arise. So why shouldn't you feel totally confident that you will succeed this time? The only thing that will prevent you from changing is hanging onto your old belief system.

Follow these four steps to overcome negative thinking and improve your sales performance.

1. Become conscious of how you think

Allocate time to observe your thoughts. You may be surprised at how many negative thoughts you have throughout the day. Don't be concerned because you are on your way to changing your selling career and your personal life. This is because you are becoming conscious of your thoughts. If a negative thought happens, notice it and then let it go. For example *"Business is really tough."* You may consider changing the statement to *"The business environment is challenging but I am up to it."*

2. Change how you think

Once you have become conscious of your negative thoughts, replace those thoughts with positive ones and always make brief matter-of-fact statements. For example, replace *"I really blew that sale"* with *"I am glad I now know where I can improve. I will ask more probing questions."* At first this targeted self-corrective thinking may feel somewhat uncomfortable but stick with it. It will have an impact on your self-worth and high self-worth individuals tend to:[4]

---

4   Everett T Robinson MA and Ken Keis MBA, 2011, **Self-Worth Inventory** CRG Consulting Resource Group International Inc

- Think better of others

- Evaluate their own performance more positively

- Work hard for people with high standards

- Influence others more often

- Act more assertively overall

- Take more personal responsibility

3. Change how you feel

This is difficult because feelings can dominate how you think. Even when you try to think positively the associated feeling might not complement the positive thought.

You need to unfreeze the negative feelings and replace them with the new desired feelings. This can be done by going through a meditation process. Sit or lie down in a quiet place with no distractions - relax, close your eyes, take a few deep breaths and exhale slowly. Then begin by visualising the outcome you want in the greatest of detail and take in the associated feelings. This is important so you experience the full effect of what you want and create an emotional shift in feelings from negative to positive. Do this repeatedly until the new thought and feelings are one and part of your new belief system.

4. Take affirmative action

Without action nothing will change. Let go of the old belief system by replacing it with a new one by actively going about your day-to-day work applying what you have learnt. It will more than likely feel uncomfortable at first but it will get easier with practice. Your persistence will pay huge dividends, both in terms of how you feel about yourself and others, and be reflected in your sales results.

As salespeople we are expected to handle rejection on a daily basis which makes it difficult, but not impossible, to remain positive. Negative thoughts can easily creep in and, left to their own devices, can take over our wellbeing. Start today by becoming conscious of your thoughts. Creating a new belief system is not an easy thing to do but it is worth every challenge so you can take control of your thinking and leading your life in a happier, healthier and more productive manner.

What Does This Chapter Mean in Your World?

1. What are the most common negative thoughts you have?

....

....

....

....

2. What effect have negative thoughts had on you?

....

....

....

....

3. What positive affirmative statements could you use?

....

....

....

....

4. What are you going to do to become more conscious of what you think?

....

....

....

....

5. When you have a negative thought how are you going to change the way you feel?

....

....

....

....

6. What actions are you going to commit to leading a positive life?

....

....

....

....

9

Sales call reluctance – what is it and what can you do if you have it?

Sales call reluctance can destroy sales careers and affect anyone, whether they are new to sales or sales veterans

_____ Thinking _____

If you haven't experienced the emotional torture of being call reluctant, the odds are you will be sooner or later. Attending motivational seminars, learning sales techniques or improving product and industry knowledge won't help you to overcome or protect you from this immobilising experience.

Researchers in the field of sales call reluctance[5] have found that it is responsible for 80% of salespeople's failure in their first year. Sales call reluctance accounts

5   George W. Dudley and Shannon L. Goodson, 2007, *The Psychology of Sales Call Reluctance*, Behavioural Sciences Research Press Inc

for over 50% of failures in the sales profession. Sadly, 40% of sales veterans think about leaving sales because they are trying to come to grips with call reluctance. The financial and emotional cost to business and to salespeople is staggering.

Sales call reluctance can be contagious because it can be passed on by sales managers, sales trainers, fellow salespeople and internal client support personnel.

What is sales call reluctance?

A sales call reluctant salesperson feels mentally and emotionally immobilised and therefore incapable of initiating new sales calls either by phone or face to face. Normal sales activities can be affected including prospecting, avoiding large group presentations and meeting with executive management, handling sales objections, and closing the sale.

The mental and emotional energy needed to sell successfully and achieve sales targets is redirected to other more comfortable and "safe" activities. These self-justifying activities are designed to spend more time in the office and can include: getting caught up talking to co-workers, busying themselves with administrative tasks, and having extended personal phone calls.

Sales call reluctance can be described as a fear of being assertive. For example, individuals do not make the urgent phone call they had planned to do and their self-talk justification can be *"I'll be intruding or possibly upset the client if I call at this time."* The salesperson believes in and acts on a self-belief that excuses them, and therefore they fail to do what they know they need to do. This self-belief creates an emotional refuge for them to hide.

There are many different forms of sales call reluctance behaviours. The most common are:

- High levels of activity but a decrease in sales results

- Sales reports contain twice the information compared to top performing salespeople

- Persistent complaints to deflect poor performance

- Seeking out like-minded people.

- Blaming others and internal systems to avoid having to take personal responsibility

- Using excuses to avoid prospecting

- Over-servicing existing clients that they feel most comfortable with.

What can you do if you are sales call reluctant?

Firstly, there is no reason to feel embarrassed or ashamed in admitting to being sales call reluctant. What is important is that you have admitted it, at least to yourself, and are now willing to change your thinking and correct falsely held beliefs that have been holding you back.

The good news is whatever triggered your sales call reluctance was learnt, and whatever was learnt can also be unlearnt. Whilst this may be challenging in the early stages, it will restore your self-respect and get your sales career back on track. By replacing sales call reluctant behaviours with positive goal-focused actions there is no room for any distractions so you will create the change you need. The proof that you are on the right track will be in the new business and increased sales you achieve. In the process you will have rediscovered your true self.

The suggested actions to overcome sales reluctance are:

1. Set meaningful goals

For goals to motivate you they need to be realistic and slightly beyond your comfort zone. If they are too high you will soon realise the gaol is impossible to achieve so you give up shortly after you begin. If the goal is too low you may think this is too easy and won't put in the effort required to achieve the outcome. Focusing on achieving your goals can be invigorating.

2. Get coaching

There are many good coaches in both executive and business coaching. However, try and find a reputable sales coach with whom you feel comfortable and can talk to openly. If they have personally been through the sales call reluctance experience then they will be of greater value to you. They will be able to truly empathise with your situation and be in a position to advise you on what they did to overcome their sales call reluctance and therefore help you to achieve your sales goals.

3. Screen your thinking

If you find yourself thinking negatively, ask yourself, *"Why am I thinking this way?"* You may discover the root cause of your sales call reluctance. Just before you meet a prospective client ask yourself *"What is the worst thing that can happen when I approach this prospective client?"* For example, *"I may be rejected and so what."* You know you will live through it. Think of how you would handle the situation behaviourally and from a skills perspective. You can also counter this thought by recalling in detail what you did in a past sales call that achieved a great outcome.

You may feel uncomfortable as you challenge your thoughts, but at least any fear you may be feeling will be lessened as you gain greater control. As you become conscious of your self-defeating thoughts, replace them with positive action and you will become more confident. You may not be able to change the situation but you do have control over your thoughts, feelings and actions.

4. Use CRM software

Client relationship management (CRM) software can help you pinpoint where you can improve. It can be revealing and highlight where you can manage sales opportunities better and confront any sales call reluctance issues.

5. Build resilience

This can be done through networking, reading books on sales and biographies written by successful people, participating in webinars on sales, and investing in your ongoing education in sales. Avoid people who are always negative — the *"yes, but…"* doom and gloom people. You may need to mentally exit or, if appropriate, excuse yourself and leave.

If you are sales call reluctant there is much you can do to help yourself. Begin by becoming conscious of any self-defeating thoughts. Don't automatically accept these thoughts as being the truth. Focus your attention on positive thoughts, feelings and actions. Find a reputable sales coach, one who will lead you back to being the successful salesperson that you have always been.

What Does This Chapter Mean in Your World?

1. What is meant by the term sales call reluctant?

....

....

....

....

2. What do you think might be possible triggers that lead to call reluctance?

....

....

....

....

3. Have you been call reluctant? If so what were your experiences?

....

....

....

....

4. What did you do to overcome your call reluctance?

....

....

....

....

5. How would you recognise a salesperson with call reluctance?

....

....

....

....

6. What would you do to help a salesperson with call reluctance?

....

....

....

....

10

Sales styles – do you know your style and what it means?

*Have you ever completed a sales call
and not understood why you didn't
get the business?*

_____ Thinking and Action _____

You review every aspect of the sales call from your approach to the close and there is nothing you can come up with that validates why the outcome was a lost sale. It's frustrating isn't it? So what went wrong? If you followed the sales process then could it be the selling style you used during the sales interview? Was the selling style different from how the client wanted to buy?

We all have our preferred way of selling that we are comfortable with, particularly if we have been selling for many years. Over time we tend to predominately use one, two or possibly three selling styles. This in itself is fine but difficulties arise when a salesperson uses a selling style that is mismatched to the way a client wants to buy.

To achieve sales success, and to maximise your sales conversion ratio, you need to identify how a client wants to buy and adapt accordingly. The skill is **style shifting**, and whilst some salespeople may think this is common sense, it isn't. **Style shifting** is a learnt skill.

The alternate to not developing style shifting skills is to find clients who buy the way you sell - or you need to have clients who are very flexible in how they buy and adapt to how you sell. Both tend to be uncommon, and whilst you may stumble across these situations, they don't occur often enough for you to achieve great sales success. This perhaps explains why some salespeople, at an unconscious level at least, call on more prospective clients than other salespeople in order to achieve at best an ordinary sales result.

Overview

There are 21 validated sales styles and each has its unique characteristic. There is no perfect sales style or one style that is better than another. However, knowing your sales style/s, the buying style of your client and the ability to style shift are skills that high performing salespeople have honed over many years. "Style shift" is the term used to describe the process of adapting sales style to the client's buying style.

The 21 sales styles are described as:

- Forceful
- Individualistic
- Committed
- Assertive
- Probing
- Investigative
- Efficient
- Astute
- Congenial
- Dependable
- Considerate
- Eager
- Enthusiastic
- Intensive
- Ingenious
- Convincing
- Persistent
- Compelling
- Venturesome
- Dynamic
- Synergistic.

So what can go wrong when a salesperson's selling style is incompatible with the client's buying style? The following brief examples are an overview only and shouldn't be interpreted as a complete list.

The *Enthusiastic* Salesperson interviewing an analytical prospect or client will tend to:

- Talk too much

- Move ahead too quickly

- Be vague with their answers.

What they should be doing is:

- Giving detailed information

- Asking for the client's or prospect's opinion

- Treating the client or prospect with respect.

The *Assertive* Salesperson interviewing a harmonious prospect or client will tend to:

- Demand they decide quickly

- Apply pressure and take advantage of the prospect's good nature

- Be impatient and show frustration or anger.

What they should be doing is:

- Being patient during the sales process

- Making the prospect feel important and effective

- Helping the prospect with important decisions.

The *Probing* Salesperson interviewing an expressive prospect or client will tend to:

- Be too task oriented

- Be overly structured

- Bore the prospect with too much detail.

What they should be doing is:

- Listening - giving them plenty of time and opportunities to speak

- Admiring their achievements

- Taking care of details for them.

The *Congenial* Salesperson interviewing a task oriented prospect or client will tend to:

- Be slow in applying the sales process

- Be passive in their presentation

- Lose control of the sales interview.

What they should be doing is:

- Giving them summarised facts as well as the big picture

- Respecting their judgments

- Cooperating with them fully.

Effective style shifting will meet a client's core needs and values. For example:

- A Cognitive (Analytical) Client has a need for order, understanding and perfection. They value quality, expertise and instruction

- A Behavioural (Action) Client has a need for achievement, power and stimulation. They value accomplishment, responsibility and challenge

- An Interpersonal (Harmony) Client has a need for appreciation, stability and unity. They value acknowledgement, security and cooperation

- An Effective (Expressive) Client has a need for attention, recreation and experience. They value recognition, pleasure and variety.[6]

If these attributes are not demonstrated by the salesperson, the client is likely to feel frustrated or possibly angry. When a salesperson doesn't style shift, they often attract sales objections. This means they now need to handle the sales objection, and deal with the emotional distractions, an objection brings to the sales interview.

Knowing how to adapt to the way a client wants to buy is a challenging skill to develop but will result in great sales success. Refer to Chapter 11: Increasing Sales through Sales Style Flexibility, to learn how to style shift.

---

6   A part extract from Ken Keis with Everett T. Robinson, 2011, *Why Aren't You More Like Me*: second edition, Friesens Corporation, Altona MB Canada

What Does This Chapter Mean in Your World?

1. What is your preferred sales style?

....

....

....

....

2. What buyer behaviour do you find the most challenging to deal with?

....

....

....

....

3. What have you done in the past to turn the client around?

....

....

....

....

4. What is the definition of style shifting?

....

....

....

....

5. What is the value in style shifting?

....

....

....

....

6. Based on what you have learnt what will you do differently when you next meet with a client?

....

....

....

....

11

Increase sales through sales style flexibility

Have you ever wondered why in some selling situations the sale comes together so effortlessly?

_____ Action _____

At other times it feels like nothing appears to come together and the outcome is a lost sale. You know that you followed the sales process, correctly applied your selling skills, and did everything right? Well so you thought.

You could put a great sales outcome down to the fact that you are a good salesperson, are well experienced, have a long-term trusting relationship with the client, and your pricing is competitive. When you don't achieve your sales objective do you use excuses such as the prospective client hadn't dealt with your company before so therefore they felt unsure... your competitor offered a larger discount or other purchasing incentives to win the business? All these reasons may or may not be true, but to get straight to the point are they really valid? The question to ask yourself is would these reasons stand up to professional scrutiny if evaluated by a third party?

Based on my experience as in sales coaching, I have found that many salespeople firmly believe they are flexible in their sales style. As stated in Chapter 10, this is the ability to adapt how a salesperson can sell the way their client or prospective client wants to buy. Generally the more inexperience salespeople will state that *"It's common sense"* when the subject of style shifting is discussed. Let's dispel this here and now. The problem with this belief is that common sense isn't used commonly and what is perceived as common sense to one person is not common sense to another. There is also the additional problem of how do you objectively evaluate a skill when common sense is so subjective? The answer is you can't.

To state the obvious, one of the core traits required to succeed in sales is the ability to influence others, in fact as many people as possible. Everyone has some flexibility, with some more than others, to influence but this is dependent on their personality, skills, motivation and attitude.

Most of us have two or three innate sales styles that we use consciously and/ or unconsciously. What this means is if we restrict ourselves to these sales styles our success will hinge on finding enough clients who will buy the way we sell. To maximise our sales success we need to develop a wider range of sales style flexibility. Being effective at applying sales skills is not enough to become a stand out sales performer.

We need to be able to identify a wider range of client buying behaviours and then intentionally shift into a selling behaviour that makes the client feel comfortable in our presence. This is easy to read and understand - but be warned, in reality it can be quite challenging because with some clients you need to implement behaviours that you have never used or very rarely use.

One of your greatest challenges is working with a client who is very task orientated. They want you to get to the point quickly, provide summarised facts, and are not interested in small talk. The sales interview that you would normally like to spend 45 minutes to an hour can be reduced to 6-7 minutes. The client will in some cases tell you to *"get on with it"* and possibly wind up the sales call if they perceive that you are too slow or are only wasting their time because there is no business value in your sales call. You are now out of your comfort zone and can feel quite tense when you can't create the environment you feel comfortable in.

By knowing how to style shift you will still feel uncomfortable but you would know how to adapt to this selling situation and be better placed to win the business.

Developing greater sales style flexibility doesn't mean you will be someone you are not - but you will learn more about yourself. This is because you are able to extend your range of behaviours, meaning you are able to effectively adapt to more people. This in turn will impact directly on your sales results.

So how do you shift your sales style? This is a three-step process:

1. Put yourself in neutral

Because we are so often rushed going from sales call to sales call we can find ourselves in an autopilot mode to get through the volume of work need in order to get the sales result. This is when we miss sales opportunities because clients who should be buying don't. There is no point in increasing the number of sales calls unless the extra activity equates to more sales. Slow down! Before your next sales call, take a deep breath, exhale slowly and relax. You have now put yourself in neutral, are out of auto pilot and have taken back control of your situation. You are no longer thinking of the previous sales call or the next one. Being in neutral is like using a manual gear box in a car - it allows you to switch to any gear instantly. From neutral you will be able to focus on identifying the buying style of the client.

2. Identify the buying style of the client

This is done by noticing the behaviours of the client during the questioning phase of the sales call. What you need to ask yourself is - is the client more task or people orientation, introverted or extroverted and verbal or non-verbal? If you have identified the client to be:

- Task orientated, extrovert and non-verbal their buying style is Action

- Task orientated, introverted and verbal their buying style is Analytical

- People orientated, introverted and non-verbal their buying style is Harmonious

- People orientated, extroverted and verbal their buying style is Expressive.

3. Shift into the right sales style

Once you have identified the client's buying style you will need to adjust your sales style.[7]

If you have identified the client's buying style as Action as a guide you will need to:

- Give them summarised facts and the big picture

- Respect their judgements

- Support them to reach specific goals

- Cope with unwanted details

- Cooperate fully with them

If you have identified the client's buying style as Analytical as a guide you will need to:

- Give them detailed information and specs

- Ask for their opinions

- Treat them with respect

- Do quality work/presentations the first time

- Not interrupt their work

If you have identified the client's buying style as Harmonious as a guide you will need to:

- Make them feel important and effective

- Be patient during the sales process

- Be kind, considerate, and thoughtful

- Help them with important decisions

- Value them as individuals

If you have identified the client's buying style as Expressive as a guide you will need to:

---

7   Terry D. Anderson, Ph.D., Ken Keis, MBA., and Bruce Wares, 2008, Sales Style Indicator, Consulting Resource Group International, Inc

- Listen; give them the opportunity to speak

- Admire their achievements

- Be influenced by them in some way

- Take care of details for them

- Value their opinions; offer alternatives

From a sales coaching perspective, I have learnt the most common reason preventing salespeople from style shifting is that they don't implement the first step in the process – putting themselves into neutral. Always start with step 1.

Selling is a competitive and demanding profession. The greatest differentiator and competitive edge you can create is having the ability to style shift and this is because many salespeople either don't know how or haven't developed style shifting skills. Possessing this skill will provide you with more effective client relationships and lead to improved sales.

What Does This Chapter Mean in Your World?

1. Why is sales style flexibility so important?

....

....

....

....

2. What is meant by the term put yourself into neutral?

....

....

....

....

3. How do you identify the buying style of a client?

....

....

....

....

4. What are the 3 steps to style shifting?

....

....

....

....

5. What is the most common reason that prevents salespeople from style shifting?

....

....

....

....

6. What selling behaviours will you need to work on to be more effective when style shifting?

....

....

....

....

12

Dealing with a difficult client complaint to ensure a positive outcome

Handling a client complaint,
either by phone or face to face,
can be a challenging task

_____ Action _____

If the complaint is highly charged with emotion and irrational statements a natural reaction would be to feel defensive and try to explain why a particular situation had occurred. This reaction can only put you on the back foot.

Research has shown that for every 25 clients who complain only one will express their thoughts and feelings directly to the organisation they hold responsible. The other 24 unhappy clients won't contact the company, but will tell 10 to 20 others about their experience. This can have a compounding effect resulting in potentially tens or possibly hundreds of prospective and existing clients being told of the situation and leaving a wake of negativity behind. The real damage, however, is the salesperson can't respond to the criticism and address it because in many instances they are not aware the complaint exists.

There are three things you can do to deal more effectively with a client complaint.

1. Don't take it personally

When listening to a client complaint, it is easy to become emotionally involved which can lead to hurt feelings, becoming annoyed or even angry. If you feel this way you may be reacting defensively rather than responding calmly to the client complaint. Being filled with emotion can only make your job of trying to resolve the problem more difficult. Emotional behaviour can project defensiveness that may manifest as a higher vocal tone and an increased speech rate. What you would be communicating to the client in this situation is that you have lost control.

When a client complains their frustration or anger is aimed at your company or the *"professional you"* and not at you personally - so welcome the complaint. It will give you the opportunity to fix the problem and open new sales opportunities in the future. Unfortunately clients who don't complain tend not to come back and, more than likely, they will tell others of their bad experience who may in turn tell more people again.

2. Acknowledge the client

Acknowledge means to recognise the client with genuine gratitude. This doesn't mean you necessarily agree with what the client has stated. Remain calm and breathe slowly to project a warm and credible vocal tone, slow down your speech rate and maintain good eye contact if this is a face to face scenario.

Acknowledge without any judgement behind it. This could be non-verbally by nodding your head or verbally with *"Aha"* in recognition of what the client has stated. Using survival phrases will let the client know that you care. For example *"I appreciate you drawing this issue to my attention"*… *"Thank you for calling to let me know"* or *"I can understand how you must be feeling."*

3. Actively listen and empathise

Unfortunately, many sales opportunities and client relationships are lost due to poor listening. This is a huge cost to business. Research shows that many people function at only 25% of their active listening capacity.

Active listening involves your full concentration on what the client is saying and feeling. It also requires you to be patient and not interrupt even if what they are saying is incorrect or you are not the right person who can solve the problem. If you did interrupt, particularly if the client is volatile, the situation will only become inflamed. When a person is filled with emotional anger they are irrational and not ready to listen to any reasonable response. They are upset and need to get what is bothering them off their chest, so you need to hear them out. After most of the emotional outburst is out of their system, they will calm down and then be ready to listen to a rational response from you. An extremely emotional outburst can last for 20 - 30 seconds.

Active listening involves 3 core skills.

- **Listening to the information**

Hearing is a passive and an automatic response. It isn't until you make a conscious effort to listen and become engaged and tune into what is being said that active listening begins.

- **Understanding the information**

You can accurately interpret what the client has said through their words, vocal tone and non-verbal gestures. You may need to paraphrase statements or questions to ensure you have fully understood what the client has said. Aim to understand the client's feelings and read between the lines. In other words, what they are really saying. Ask if you can take notes as taking notes will slow down the process and the client's anger will soften quicker because they will see that you really care by trying to get all the facts.

- **Assessing the information**

Whether you agree or disagree with what has been stated, don't react by jumping to any conclusion. Remain calm and don't change your demeanour. The information could be incomplete or filtered through their perception or bias.

When you are in doubt ask more questions or paraphrase. This is an opportunity for you to take control, reduce the client's anger and building rapport. These multiple outcomes are possible because when you ask open questions you will encourage the client to speak freely. This in turn will provide you with the information you need. As the client is speaking they will also be releasing their negative feelings relating to the problem. They will then be ready to listen to you. By showing that you care for the client through actively listening and asking open questions, the client will respond in a positive manner.

Research has shown that 68% of clients won't buy from the same person or company again because they feel that they don't care.

- **Responding to the information**

Your verbal and non-verbal feedback needs to communicate that you have listened, understood and accurately assessed what the client has told you. This will create mutual understanding. Inappropriate responses include reacting defensively or aggressively, and remaining silent and not responding.

Once you have all the information you need you will be in a position to solve the client's problem. Sometimes it can be straightforward and other times more complex. In these situations why not ask the client what they think would be a fair solution? You may be surprised that the client's answer could be less costly than the one you may be considering. For example, *"Mary, if you were in my shoes what would you do to resolve this issue?"*

Once a solution has been agreed upon, it's important to ask for the client's feedback. This way you can be sure that the client is satisfied with the solution. You might ask, *"If I were to agree with your suggestion, would you be happy with that? or "That takes care of that, doesn't it?"*

4. Follow up

Follow up is often not consistently done by companies and in some cases not at all. A phone call or send a thank you card in the mail can communicate much about you to the client. It is an opportunity to differentiate yourself and your company from competitors, and it will help you to build loyal and long term client.

If a complaint has been handled well, from the client's perspective, 91% of clients will come back and buy again. In fact, they will feel a closer connection because of the emotional experience they shared with you. The client knows that if in the future there is a problem it isn't really a problem because they know you will look after them and follow up ensuring all is well. Following up may also lead to your being given referred business.

Dealing with difficult clients can be an uncomfortable experience. But taking a professional approach and responding rationally, actively listening and not getting emotionally entangled will help you to remain objective and therefore be in a better position to resolve any problem.

What Does This Chapter Mean in Your World?

1. What have been the most difficult client complaints you have had?

....

....

....

....

2. What were some of the mistakes you made in handling those complaints?

....

....

....

....

3. What problems arise when a complaint is taken personally?

....

....

....

....

4. What are the 3 core skills to active listening?

....

....

....

....

5. What are the benefits of follow up?

....

....

....

6. What did you learnt that will be of greatest value to you?

....

....

....

....

13

Follow up - why is it so important and yet done so poorly?

Following up is an easy and straightforward task, yet it isn't common practice in sales

_____ Action _____

The first question to ask is indeed why? Why isn't follow up implemented as part of the sales process and used as naturally as we breathe air? By not following up, sales are lost and opportunities to build client relationships are hindered.

The reason why salespeople don't follow up can broadly fall into one or more of 3 categories:

1. Don't know

The salesperson was not told that follow up is part of their job and why it is important. If the salesperson realised the value and the 'feel good' connection it can create between themselves and the client, every salesperson would want to do it.

The reason for not knowing is the salesperson has not been trained correctly, or at all, on how to follow up. Reviewing past client sales training courses I have been surprised by the amount of time that follow up was not part the course. At best, some had listed suggestions of what to do but not the reasons why follow up is so integral to sales.

2. Make assumptions

This is when a salesperson assumes a certain outcome has or will occur. For example, this could be that the client is satisfied, happy, will call back, the product will perform the way it was designed to, or if there is an issue they will contact customer service. All of these reasons could be true or not true but why not take control and find out rather than do nothing and/or leaving the responsibly to someone else?

Follow up can be to ensure a delivery happened within an agreed time, to gather feedback on the product's performance, or to monitor the outcome of a management meeting that reviewed your proposal. Call or, better still, meet with the client in person to do this. particularly if it is a delicate situation.

A common assumption is when the salesperson emailed a proposal and they assume the client will call back when they are ready. The lack of follow up in this case can invite problems, one of which is that the client may give the business to a competitor because they think you just don't care.

An important foot note: avoid emailing proposals - always present them in person. If you do not, you will have no control of the clients understanding of the proposal and you are not there to answer any questions and proactively overcome objections.

3. Fear

As salespeople, we all have to cope with fear. It is part of our job and perhaps is the reason why we entered the sales profession…to be challenged? If not addressed, fear can immobilise and destroy a sales career.

Fear is often low self-worth created by falsely held beliefs. The self-talk that could lead to not following up are:

- The client will only say no

- It's too early or too it's late now

- I was unsuccessful the last time

- We don't have much of a chance

- They will only criticise me and/or the proposal

- I will only be intruding (and don't want to feel uncomfortable)

- It's not that important

Develop the habit

Follow-up can be in person, by phone, SMS or email. By setting up another appointment at the conclusion of a sales call can progress a sales opportunity. Follow-up can be to call back with information or simply to thank the client. Whatever follow up method is used it creates an opportunity to reconnect with the client.

Effective follow up is done only 25% of the time, so executed well it can provide an opportunity for you to differentiate yourself from your competitors, generate referral business, create high retention of clients, and grow repeat business. There is no down side to follow up.

Developing an organised and systematic approach to following up, whether you use a manual diary or the latest CRM tool, does not matter as long as the system supports what you are aiming to achieve. Make sure follow up becomes part of your daily selling activities as it will help you to build strong client relationships and sales.

The follow-up client categories are:

1. The referral

Contacting a referred lead in itself does not guarantee a sale but it is often easier than starting from scratch. Studies show that experienced salespeople reduce their selling time by 50-95% when working with a referred, verses a non-referred, sales opportunity. They also keep the referrer updated with progress and outcomes of the referred prospect. This is not only the courteous thing to do but often leads to the referrer giving you more referrals.

You can find more information on referrals by reading Chapter 16 – The

Smart Way to Prospect to Generate New Business.

2. The new client

Following-up on a new client can be an enjoyable and an exciting experience. It can provide opportunities to ask for their feedback, uncover other issues you may be able to help them solve, and build your creditability in addition to that of your company's.

3. The angry client

Following-up on an angry or irate client can be an uncomfortable experience but contacting the client needs to be done with urgency. If it is serious enough, this should really be done in person. I am sure you will have experienced what it feels like not to have been contacted after you have complained about a product or service purchase, so contacting the client urgently is not only the right thing to do but it is good business practice to do so. The client may be surprised to hear or see you but will appreciate your follow-up and the courage to 'face the music', as can be the case at times. In this situation, ask questions to identify their level of dissatisfaction, for example, are they extremely upset of just unhappy? This will help you come up with the right answers and response rate to correct the problem. Aim to finish the call or personal visit on a positive note and always thank them for their feedback.

4. The loyal client

Unfortunately loyal clients can often be taken for granted and, in the great majority of cases, will end up with a competitor having been given the business. In this situation, companies then tend to go into overdrive to win the business back but rarely do they succeed and if so at vastly reduced profit margins. If you have a loyal client who has given you a lot of business, then let them know regularly how much you truly value them - and not when it's too late. By doing so, you will develop a closer working relationship and, in many instances, automatically lock out competitors.

It doesn't matter what category of client you are dealing with - always, always follow-up. Don't give it a second though - just do it. Follow up needs to be a non-negotiable part of the sales process and will help you to build client relationships and sales for now and the future.

What Does This Chapter Mean in Your World?

1. What excuses have you heard, or perhaps used yourself, for not following up?

....

....

....

....

2. Whenever you hadn't followed up what problems occurred?

....

....

....

....

3. What do you believe are the most common reasons why salespeople don't follow up?

....

....

....

....

4. What are the 4 client follow up categories?

....

....

....

....

5. Outline what you would say to a client when asking for a hot referral?

....

....

....

....

6. What are you going to commit to doing to ensure you follow up?

....

....

....

....

14

How to reduce the selling cycle

*The selling cycle is a time frame
that is measured from the initial client contact
to confirmation of the business*

_____ Action _____

Focusing only on the selling cycle is common practice but is a flawed strategy. This is because we only have control over our sales activities and not the sale per se — the client has. Believing we have control can create relationship and credibility issues as well as problems in closing the sale. Why? Because the client feels they are being pushed into buying now rather than having decided themselves to buy now. This is pressuring the client to work within the salesperson's selling timeframe rather than theirs.

When a client is in the market for a product or service they go through a buying process, and whilst it is different from the selling process it remains a process nonetheless. Problems occur when these two processes are not aligned. However, when correctly aligned, the time it takes to get new business confirmed is reduced and, in turn, it makes your job easier and the client experience more enjoyable.

Before we look at how to create *"process synergy"* it's important we understand what the common problems are that affect buying and selling cycles.

Factors that can extend the buying cycle are:

• Having no previous dealings with your company and/or unfamiliarity with your products or services

• More people getting involved in the decision process, which slows momentum and increases the risk of procrastination meaning the sales opportunity is lost.

• Decisions that require a substantial financial commitment

• Having cross-organisational functions involved in the decision process

• Bidding for the same business by competitors, including a client's internal resources

• Having other client needs competing for the same funding

• Fear of a personal backlash for making the wrong decision or recommendation. In this situation, the safest option is to do nothing because any other action would be perceived as too risky

The best way to sort and manage sales opportunities, and also the selling cycle, is to use a sales funnel. However, problems can occur when:

•   Standardisation isn't implemented, or compliance of the sales funnel is not adhered to. Different interpretations of what has to be done, plus limited or no client information, makes client management and accurate sales forecasting impossible. This also means the salesperson has all the client information mentally, so should they leave the company, they take the client intelligence with them.

• Sales opportunities that should be removed are left in the sales funnel. This is usually because of poor qualification, ignorance, or the desire to show an impressive sales funnel. Sooner or later the truth will emerge when forecasted sales targets are not met

• There is no focus on what can be closed now

• There is too much reliance on sales to existing clients and failure to regularly prospect for new business

- There is a lack of prioritising sales opportunities

- Too much time is spent on low value sales opportunities

The sales funnel is used to manage current sales opportunities in the selling cycle. The traditional weighted funnel that consists of percentages based on probability can be too subjective and therefore ineffective.

There are 4 tiers to measure the selling activity:

Tier 0 – Uncover

The sales activity for this tier is to implement a range of prospecting initiatives such as networking and asking for referred leads to uncover potential new sales.

Tier 1 – Sales Opportunity

This tier requires qualification of the sales opportunity by interviewing the client, identifying all the people involved in the decision process, and qualifying the product or service need.

Tier 2 – Advance

Advance is to build your influence with the key people involved in the decision making process and your knowledge of the client organisation. This also requires that you uncover the selection criteria for your product or service.

Tier 3 – Confirm

The activity for this last tier is to get confirmation of the sale. If a formal proposal was presented, it would have been done during Tier 2 with all those involved in the decision process.

So what can you do to align the buying and selling processes?

The buying cycle has a four-stage process described as **concealed, awareness, analysis** and **decision**.

1. Concealed

This means the client isn't aware a problem exists or they choose to ignore it for whatever reason. Sometimes problems are hidden from the client, particularly in larger organisations. The problem is usually exposed when there is a large cost or cash flow issue. The concealed stage is in line with Tier 0 of the sales funnel – Uncover.

2. Awareness

This is when the client becomes conscious of the problem or new possibilities, and realises that they need to do something about it. The type of problem and its impact on the business will determine whether they will take any action. Some problems, whilst being an annoyance, may not be worth investing time and money to address. Qualifying and quantifying the full extent of the problem as it relates to your product or services will put you in a position to help the client. The awareness stage is in line with Tier 1 of the sales funnel – The Sales Opportunity.

3. Analysis

Analysis involves the client looking at all options available to them including their internal resources and other potential suppliers. This is a natural part of the buying process and one that some salespeople find annoying, so they become impatient. Stay close and show your support by informing and answering questions for those involved in the decision process. Don't fall into the trap of becoming pushy or over-selling. The analysis stage is in line with Tier 2 of the sales funnel – Advance.

4. Decision

If you have a good existing client relationship where trust and credibility have been well established, you will more than likely get the business confirmed quickly. However, if you don't have a track record with the client and there are difficult economic conditions, then you could be at a disadvantage because clients will tend to stay with suppliers they have previously used. The decision stage is in line with Tier 3 of the sales funnel – Confirm.

During the decision stage of the buying process you need to be attentive to any last-minute concerns that may need to be addressed. Any complacency on your part could risk losing the sale.

When you align your selling cycle with the client's buying cycle you will automatically reduce the time involved to get the sale confirmed. Your credibility will also be enhanced because you will be seen as someone who is in step with how the client wants to buy.

In Summary:

Selling Activity	Buying Process
Tier 0 – Uncover	Concealed
Tier 1 – Sales Opportunity	Awareness
Tier 2 – Advance	Analysis
Tier 3 – Confirm	Decision

What Does This Chapter Mean in Your World?

1. What problems have you experienced when the selling cycle was out of sync with the client's buying cycle?

....

....

....

....

2. List 3 factors that can extend the buying cycle

....

....

....

....

3. What have been some of the problems you have experienced with ineffective sales funnels?

....

....

....

....

4. List the 4 tiers to measure selling activity

....

....

....

....

5. What are the 4 stages of the buying cycle?

....

....

....

....

6. What has been the most valuable lesson you have learnt in this chapter?

....

....

....

....

15

Why selling and buying cycles can be out of sync

*Have you ever walked out of a sales call thinking
'This is a sure thing' only to be disappointed
later when you learn the business
went to a competitor?*

_____ Thinking _____

So what went wrong? Could it have been the cost, a competitor had a better product or service, or the competing salesperson was more competent? (Ouch!)

Whilst these reasons are possible in a complex sale, the most common cause for having lost the sale is the selling cycle is out of sync with the client's buying cycle. So how does this happen? Most often it's because the salesperson has developed a sales strategy in isolation to the client's buying strategy which results in a mismatch and therefore the sales opportunity is lost.

In the previous chapter on how to reduce the selling cycle, we said that both buying and selling are processes. So if you know your sales process, then it's only a matter of learning the client's buying process and where they are at any given time in their process. Using the four stages, let's recap and add one extra stage: the Evaluation.

1. Concealed

If the client doesn't know or refuses to acknowledge that a problem exists, then nothing happens. It is not uncommon for others in the organisation to be aware of a problem and not act for reasons only known to themselves. However, these people can be of great value to you because they have not only identified the problem but will know the impact it has on areas such as productivity, morale and the organisation. This information can help you to build your business case.

2. Awareness

When the client has identified or acknowledged a problem exists, preferably one that is causing great concern and is costly to the organisation, they will need to act to solve it. Your role in the client awareness stage is to uncover the full extent of the problem and its effect by asking probing questions. This will clarify the seriousness of the problem for the client and that they will need to do something about it urgently.

3. Analysis

Analysis involves the client looking at all the options available including screening potential suppliers and internal resources.

In today's competitive selling environment, clients are taking longer during this stage of their buying cycle. It is tempting to move this stage along quicker by offering an inducement such as a discount. The risk is that you could be perceived as pressuring the client and you would be giving away profit margin which could have little or no effect on reducing the time frame.

During this stage:

• Find out what the client will be basing their selection criteria on. For example, client support within an agreed time

- Get agreement to extend the selection criteria to include an item that is a company strength but may have been missed by the client. For example, regular sales calls within the client's network of branches

- Highlight the close match that exists between your product or service and the items on their selection criteria.

When assessing and choosing a supplier, clients use selection criteria that can be categorised as essential and non-essential. They also use this to compare the advantages and disadvantages of each proposal. For example, the selection criteria might be service and low cost.

Some clients will place weighted scores on each criterion particularly when a major decision will need to be made. A perfect match between the selection criteria and the successful proposal is highly unlikely, so some negotiation is required. Your success will be based on achieving the closest match between the client's selection criteria and your proposal.

Common strategy mistakes in achieving the closest match between your proposal and the client's selection criteria include:

- Failing to ask the right questions to uncover the selection criteria

- Assuming the selection criteria

- An inability to modify or extend the selection criteria to include another item so it is more closely matched to the sales proposal

- A misalignment between a selling and buying cycle stage

- Failure to highlight key client selection criteria with significant product or service value.

It can be challenging and even difficult to achieve a successful outcome in the analysis stage. The reason for this can be the number of people involved and their individual motives including their possible resistance to change. Competitor influence is also part of the mix.

You can try to change one or more of the selection criteria by using the following strategies:

- Highlight to the client how your product or service meets their selection criteria. Encourage interaction and provide good business reasons for the client to use the selection criteria when they make their decision

- Reaffirm your product or service and its compatibility with at least one essential criterion

• Increase the value of the criterion that is believed to be less essential. It may have been missed previously and should be revisited.

Strategies that can work are:

• Negotiating and offering something different that's still in-line with the client's criteria

• Showing how other criteria are equally important

• Expanding the criteria to include others to take the focus off those you can't meet or don't do well. This is the most risky and most difficult strategy and needs to be used with great care.

Gaining a competitive advantage through differentiation

To qualify as a differentiator, it must come from the client's perspective and not yours. The value of the differentiator must be measurable and one that your competitor, including the client's internal resources, cannot replicate or easily replicate. An example is superior client service.

The two types of differentiators are **tangible** and **intangible**.

Tangible differentiators

Clients can easily measure tangible differentiators; for example, a specification. If your product or service includes a tangible differentiator which is in the client's selection criteria, your proposal will be in a good position to win the business. Clients will often rely on tangible differentiators particularly when they need to make a quick decision.

Intangible differentiators

These can be difficult but not impossible for clients to measure because of the very nature of an intangible differentiator, so they may avoid using them. For example, measuring the level of commitment to client service.

Clients are increasingly looking at differentiators to make their decisions. The importance they place on tangible or intangible differentiators, and how these align or don't align with your proposal, will determine the outcome and speed at which a decision is made to proceed.

4. Decision

During the Analysis stage, price will appear to be an important factor. This will be less important if the risk of doing business with you is less of a risk than doing business with your competitors.

Clients will tend to stay with suppliers whom they have a track record with and can trust. If the client becomes concerned prior to making the final decision, it will need to be addressed. Concerns can be hidden and difficult to uncover. Unresolved concerns, either real or perceived, can cost a sale. If the sale is lost to a competitor, the client will more than likely use the excuse of cost being the reason because this may appear more acceptable.

Potential concerns

Any of the following situations can present a hidden concern:

- Price hypersensitivity – this is when the client has unrealistic cost expectations and questions every aspect of your pricing

- Cancelled and rescheduled appointments – this is an indicator that there are other issues that need to be uncovered

- Rehash of a past issue – the client keeps referring to a resolved issue as if it were not resolved

- Refusal to give information – basic information is kept from you because it is treated as if it were highly confidential.

Handling concerns

The following are useful guidelines:

- The client will be more open and prepared to discuss any concerns they may have if the relationship is built on trust and honesty

- Ask questions in a warm and caring manner about what appears to be their concern

- If the client has a fear of making the wrong decision, then reassure them that they are making the right decision

- Don't use high pressure selling tactics and be patient.

5. Evaluation

Once your company has delivered on the product or service, the client will evaluate its performance. When the client receives the promised outcome, opportunities exist for you to establish a closer business relationship that can result in add-on sales, the introduction of new products and services. This will also block the entry of your competitors.

The three phases of evaluation are **expectation**, **experience** and **exit**.

i) **Expectation**. Expectation occurs prior to the supply or implementation of the product or service. It can be an exciting time for the client because they may have had the problem for some time and are now looking forward to having it fixed and enjoying the benefits.

ii) **Experience**. The company needs to deliver what it promised and is expected by the client. During the analysis stage it's important to ensure that the client doesn't have expectations that are unrealistic. The client's experience will depend on two factors:

• Their level of commitment to change brought about by your product or service

• How well your product or service is implemented in the client's organisation.

iii) **Exit**. When a successful outcome has been achieved it's time to exit. It can also be a time of reflection for both parties on what went well and any difficulties that were overcome. Hopefully it will be a time of celebration.

The Selling Cycle

The selling cycle can be affected when:

• The client hasn't previously dealt with your company and is unfamiliar with your product or services

• A major decision is required that will need a large financial outlay

• Cross-organisational functions are involved in the decision process

• Many competitors including the client's internal resources are bidding for the same business

• Other client needs are competing for the same funding

- Fear of making the wrong decision or recommendation

- Internal politics.

Sales pipeline difficulties

In this current economic climate, the sales pipeline can be difficult to fill with quality sales opportunities. This is due to two reasons:

- Clients leave the need to begin their buying cycle until it is really necessary. This affects the number of prospects you have in your pipeline

- The time taken to progress from Awareness to Decision is taking longer because more time is spent in the Analysis stage.

Sales opportunities don't progress or exit the sales pipeline because:

- They are not qualified properly, so the number of opportunities is high but going no where

- The sales pipeline is not being managed effectively

- The client procrastinates, so the sales opportunity is stuck.

Note: When the selling cycle is extended well beyond the norm there is the real risk it will fall over.

Developing a sales strategy that complements a client's buying cycle will create a point of difference, reduce your selling cycle time and will help you to close more sales more often.

What Does This Chapter Mean in Your World?

1. List 3 common strategy mistakes and any personal experiences you have had

....

....

....

....

2. Name 1 of 3 strategies you could use to change a client's selection criteria

....

....

....

....

3. What intangible differentiator have you or could you use?

....

....

....

....

4. What hidden client concerns have you uncovered?

....

....

....

....

5. List 3 factors that can affect the selling cycle

....

....

....

6. What has been the most valuable lesson you have learnt in this chapter?

....

....

....

....

16

The smart way to prospect to generate new business

There are four main reasons
why salespeople don't prospect for new business

_____ Thinking and Action _____

These are:

1. It doesn't feel comfortable

Most salespeople don't like to prospect. Decision makers can be hard to reach even after multiple phone call attempts and after many messages have been left. Prospecting can be very repetitive and tiring, for example, a sales role may require 4 to 5 hours per day, every day, hunting for new business door to door or on the phone. The rejection rate is often high and in situations where there is no direct rejection the level of indifference from a prospect can be taxing. Unless a salesperson is motivated to continue on their current path because they will achieve a substantial income from this activity, they will soon give up.

2. Don't know how

Some mangers assume that because they have hired a salesperson, the salesperson knows how to prospect. Not being able to prospect, or ineffective prospecting, is a common problem, particularly for the inexperienced salesperson. This situation can lead to the first reason for not wanting to prospect - it just does not feel comfortable.

3. It is not measured by the company

If prospecting activity isn't measured, quite frankly it won't get done, or at best a minimal amount of time is allocated to it. Only measuring sales revenue without addressing how a sale was generated will lead to the sales pipeline drying up. If current repeat business is relied upon as the only source of income, over time this will also diminish because of natural market pressures such as business closures, mergers, or a newly appointed buyer/decision maker prefers to deal with another supplier.

4. It isn't part of the sales process

Prospecting is a time consuming activity and, with many daily sales tasks needing to be performed, it is easy to get side tracked or avoid it. Prospecting has to be integral to your role and done consistently with regular time needing to be set aside for it. There are many prospecting options available, and do depend on the industry, type of sales, and the size of the company you work for, and include: lead enquiries from your company's website; a marketing campaign; networking; internal sources such a customer service/telemarketing; or by an external provider of leads. There are also proactive prospecting methods that could be part of your sales process, such as going door to door, phoning, email or sending an introductory letter by mail and then following up.

Prospecting is looking for new sales opportunities and sorting these opportunities that are genuine from those that are a waste of time.

There are many ways to prospect as previously mentioned and you need to implement those that work for you. The fact is, the newer the prospect is to you, your company and its products, the more people you need to speak to within the prospective client organisation as they will all have a direct bearing on lengthen of the selling cycle.

This is why referral business is the most effective way to acquire new clients and create sales growth. When a client gives you a referral it is personal, and being personal, their credibility and trustworthiness is transferred to you. Often in this situation, the prospective client will tend not to shop around for comparative costs and therefore the selling cycle can be reduced and lock out your competitors. Generating new sales by working this way is also very enjoyable.

There are salespeople who don't ask for, and therefore generate, enough referral business meaning the opportunities lost are huge. For example, a major US stockbroker surveyed its best clients and asked if they would be willing to refer their stockbroker. The response was positive in 84% of cases. Yet when the firm asked their brokers the percentage of time they asked their clients for referrals the answer was only 15%.

In our experience, salespeople who actively and consistently pursue referrals can earn more than 4 times the income than those who don't ask.

Developing referrals

Referrals can be found in many different areas including; from key people within the client organisation, dormant accounts, past influential co-workers, and social media (including friends and business contacts on Facebook, LinkedIn or other sites). The quality of your relationship will depend on how long you have known the individual, how often you have been in contact, and, if they are a client, how satisfied they are with you personally, your product and/or service.

Remember, referrals can be either hot or cold. A hot referral is one where the prospective client knows who you are and is expecting your call. This is as a direct result of the relationship with the referring client having been built over a long period of time and a solid track record established. In essence, you have asked the right questions to set up the hot referral.

On the other hand, a cold referral is one where the prospective client does not know you and is not expecting your call. This often occurs because the referring client does not know you that well and therefore could feel uncomfortable to refer you in the manner you would like. Sometimes they may simply give you a name and number. In some cases they could tell you not to use their name. The other reason for the cold referral is you may not have had the proper training in asking the right questions of course. A cold referral has limited value and, unfortunately, is more common that a hot referral.

Measure your referral prospecting by keeping a record of the number of people you have approached, those that converted to a hot and cold referral, the number of face to face meetings, and the number of sales and sales revenue you have achieved. You can then compare these figures with other forms of prospecting. If the sales revenue from other prospecting activities is less, this does not automatically mean you stop the activity. Some require more time and patience to achieve the outcome you are aiming for. For example, networking at a business chamber can take many months of attending functions before you are known and will take longer to develop trust and creditability.

Where to start?

Write a list of everyone you know that could have direct and indirect prospect value, including downloading all of your social media contacts, then:

1. Prioritise the list from best to least known.

2. Diarise an equal number of people to contact every week and aim to meet them in person wherever possible.

3. Let them know you would like to grow your sales through referrals and briefly describe the profile of your ideal client. Then ask for one to two names that fit the profile.

4. Ask qualifying questions and contact details.

Examples include *"Why do you think they would be interested?"*, *"How long does it usually take to get approval of this type?"* and *"Who makes the decisions?"*

5. Ask the referee to make the introduction by phone, email or in person if appropriate.

For example, *"Sam would you mind calling Mary and introducing me so she will expect my call and know what it is about?"*

6. Thank them.

7. After the referral has been contacted, let the person who referred you know the outcome. This shows courtesy and can lead to many more referrals being given.

When a prospective client becomes a client, they will tend to refer others to you because that is how they were introduced to you.

Growing sales through referrals saves time and is an enjoyable way to work, develop new business opportunities, and create sales growth. It's also more profitable and can give you a competitive edge.

What Does This Chapter Mean in Your World?

1. What are the 4 main reasons why salespeople don't prospect for business?

....

....

....

....

2. Have you ever, or do you currently avoid prospecting?
If so what excuses do you tell yourself? What will you do to change your thinking?

....

....

....

....

3. What are the potential difficulties in getting cold referrals?

....

....

....

4. What benefits are there in developing hot referrals?

....

....

....

....

5. Write a full list of names that you could approach to prospect

....

....

....

....

6. Write in your own words what you will commit to doing to develop hot referrals

....

....

....

....

17

Questioning – the foundation of selling

We can learn much from a doctor's questioning skills

_____ Thinking and Action _____

For example, even though you may have a minor flu symptom, the doctor will still ask a series of logical questions such as, *"How long have you had these symptoms?"*, *"Do you have a sore throat?"* and *"Do you have a headache?"* When a doctor thinks they have pinpointed the problem they will ask more specific questions relating to the illness. These questions are designed so that they can reach a clear understanding of the symptoms. This process precedes any diagnosis, and when the type of flu has been identified it enables the doctor to talk about what the symptoms mean and what can be done to relieve the pain or discomfort.

Yet in sales why do we so often try and "wing" questioning? Is it through ignorance or arrogance? Back to the doctor analogy, how would you feel if a doctor asked very few questions and immediately started writing a script and then told you what to do? Would you feel that they may have incorrectly diagnosed the symptoms because not enough time was spent asking questions…that you hadn't got your money's worth…feel a bit apprehensive?

We have all been guilty of rushing into a presentation without having asked enough questions. From the client's perspective, the questioning phase of the sales process was but a brief moment followed by a long-winded presentation. Not asking enough of the right questions often leads to sales objections later in the sales call and then we wonder why.

The skill of asking questions is one of the most powerful skills we can develop because through questioning we direct the thinking of the client. The language we use when we ask a question will affect how the client feels, thinks and responds.

Questioning can be used to build rapport and uncover business issues. Respectively these could be *"How did you get involved in the coaching of the junior football team?"* and *"What effect has losing your warehouse manager had on the business and the workload of other employees?"*

Showing a genuine interest in the client's current situation and the effect it has on their company and the employees can be a powerful differentiator. Questioning is used to:

- Uncover what the client needs are

- Understand if other people need to be involved in the decision process

- Clarify if the product or service has been budgeted for or that they can afford it.

A clients' motivation to buy is either to avoid a loss or to gain pleasure. Questioning can uncover current problems or ones that have been ignored for some time. Asking the right questions will evoke an emotional response or reaction. Problems are usually centred on a need to reduce operational costs and or to improve profitability.

PIE questioning, an acronym for **Profile**, **Issue** and **Effect**, is designed to help you to uncover specific needs that when bought to the surface will motivate the client to do something about it.

Profile Questions

Sources for profile questions are within the client's organisation and can be of an operational or personal nature. Profile questions are open questions that are broad in nature and are aimed at probing to find existing or potential problems. For example: *"How many company reports are printed annually?"*, *"How would you describe your current business environment?"* and *"How many contractors are on jobs per day?"* Using a simile, profile questions are like a flat rock skimming across a lake. The rock hits many points of the surface of the water but eventually it sinks. The sinking represents acknowledgement of a problem by the client.

To avoid asking too many profile questions:

- Set clear sales call objectives

- Find basic information from other sources such as Google and LinkedIn

- Pre-plan questions that are directly linked to the existing or potential problem.

Issue Questions

Issue questions take the profile question to a deeper level by asking questions directly about the client's existing or potential problem they acknowledged. The client becomes more emotionally engaged in the conversation when more issue rather than profile questions are asked. Examples in keeping with the previous profile questions could be: *"What are the main obstacles to getting the reports printed on time?"*, *"What difficulties has the current business environment created?"* and *"What are some of your key challenges to increasing the number of contractors?"*

Issue questions can:

- Narrow the scope of questions you need to ask

- Create greater understanding of the problem

- Provide you with the effect question/s you need to ask.

Effect Questions

Effect questions are about the consequences or outcomes of the client's existing or potential problem and can confirm for the client that they need to take action. The greater the gap between the cost of the problem to the organisation and/or the personal stress compared to the cost of your solution, the quicker the client will be motivated to buy. If the client's response is lukewarm, then they won't be motivated to change. In this situation go back to asking profile questions or issue questions along a different problem path.

Following on from the previous issue questions: *"What are the consequences for late delivery of the reports?"*, *"How has the current business environment affected your sales revenues?"* and *"If you were not able to increase the number of contractors, what impact would that have on your company?"*

Effect questions can:

- Provide a complete picture of the problem and its full effect

- Show a cause and effect that impact other problems

- Lead to clarity of what is specifically needed.

Client Motivation to Buy

It is a natural for a client to want to avoid pain and to feel good. An increase in pain in the present or near future is one of the main drivers that will motivate a client into action quickly. This then begins the buying process.

A client will be motivated to buy in two out of three of the following situations:

1. Dormant Pain

This is when the client isn't aware of or denies there is a problem. When not knowing all the facts or rationalising the need for change nothing will happen. Prospective clients can often fall into this category. An example would be a client putting up with an unreliable supplier because of the fear of change. If, however, there is genuine potential for future sales, then work on developing the relationship because sooner or later the client will go into acknowledging their pain.

2. Acknowledged Pain

This is when the client has admitted to a problem or a need and is looking for a solution. Acknowledged pain can have twice the motivating power to act compared to that of desire. Statements made by the client could be: *"I have a problem with…"*, *"I am looking for a better way to…"*, and *"We need to urgently fix…"*

3. Desire the Future

This category is when the client can clearly visualise the future using your product or service and become emotionally connected to the desired state. The brighter the future, the greater the desire and the need to act immediately become very apparent to the client. For example, lower costs and recognition for a job well done by their peers.

PIE Questioning in summary:

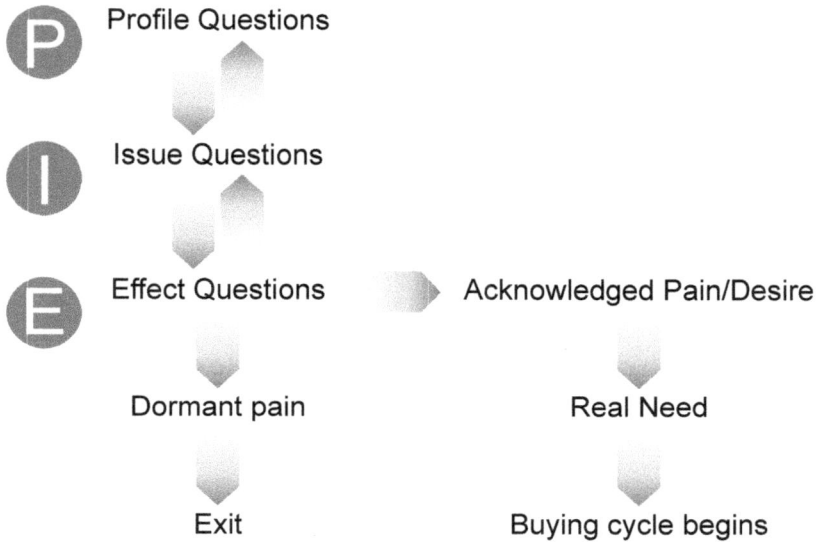

P Profile Questions

I Issue Questions

E Effect Questions → Acknowledged Pain/Desire

Dormant pain → Real Need

Exit → Buying cycle begins

PIE questioning can help to differentiate you from competing salespeople and understand the full extent of the client's problem. This in turn enables you to recommend the right product or service, and closing the sale is often driven by the client.

What Does This Chapter Mean in Your World?

1. What has been the outcome of a past sales opportunity when you didn't ask enough of the right questions?

....

....

....

....

2. What is your understanding of a Profile Question?
Provide an example relating to your product or service

....

....

....

....

3. What is your understanding of an Issue Question?
Provide an example relating to your product or service

....

....

....

4. What is your understanding of an Effect Question? Provide an example relating to your product or service

....

....

....

....

5. Name the two client motivations to buy and why they can progress a sales opportunity

....

....

....

....

6. What will you commit to doing to develop PIE Questioning Skills?

....

....

....

....

18

Sales objections – good or bad?

Let's face it: no one likes to hear
a sales objection

_____ Thinking and Action _____

Sales objections are a barrier, an excuse or a verbal defence not to buy. Depending on the volume of contact with prospective clients in any day, it can feel, at least at times, like you are constantly being rejection. All of us do not like to feel rejected but in sales it is part of the job.

What is a sales objection?

A sales objection is an explicit statement made by the client that is a barrier between their current situation and one that you know could be of benefit to them personally or to their business. When a sales objection is given there is a degree of frustration and possibly anger felt by the client. This means that both the sales objection itself and the associated emotion need to be addressed in order for the person to feel at ease again.

The old school of selling taught that sales objections were an indicator of a client's interest. In fact, they advocated that the more sales objections given, the greater the chance of securing the sale. This is completely false. Sales objections impede sales and can stifle a client relationship.

Sales objections are an indicator that something is not right. It could be that one or more skills within the sales process were poorly applied or the client wasn't fully engaged and didn't listen. Whatever the reason for the objection, it provides you with an opportunity for corrective action so the client and you are in alignment. Sales objections are a temporary business refusal and therefore are not to be taken as personal rejection.

If sales objections are given in succession it is a warning that there is something seriously wrong between the client and you, and this needs to be addressed urgently. We do not overcome sales objections - the client does, but only if we guide them through this process.

Common Sales Objections:

- Price - *"You are too expensive."*

- Thinking time - *"We haven't bought this before so we will need to think about it."*

- No Money – *"We have spent our allocated budget this year."*

- Already has it - *"We have stocks of a similar product"* or, *"Have commissioned someone to do the work."*

- Information – *"Leave me with a brochure."*

- Past experience - *"I don't like dealing with your company."*

What can you do?

Sales objections can, to a large extent, be prevented by a more effective implementation of selling skills, particularly questioning. A sales objection is not the same as a rebuttal. The difference is that a rebuttal occurs during the first few moments of connecting with a client. An example is, *"I am too busy."* A sales objection is given at the later stage of the sales process, often after the presentation. For example, a poorly qualified client could object by saying *"It's too expensive"* to *"I want to think about it"* because they don't have the authority to proceed.

How to handle a sales objection

Focusing on only overcoming the sales objection without addressing the client's feelings will result in more objections.

A proven method for working through a sales objection is AQA – FM. This is an acronym for Acknowledge, Question, Answer, Feedback and Move on.

Acknowledge

Don't react to a sales objection even if it a false statement because any tension or disappointment will show. Respond by actively listening in a non-judgemental manner and acknowledge positively, either verbally or non-verbally. For example; *"I see"*, *"I understand"* or non-words such as *"aha"* and *"hmm."* Don't begin with the word *"but"* because it can be interpreted as dismissing what the client has just said. For example, by saying "I appreciate where you are coming from but…" the client will focus on what comes after the word 'but', which is the part they don't really want to hear. Non-verbal communication could be nodding your head, making good eye contact and leaning slightly forward. This will show the client that you have empathy and have understood what they have said. It will also project confidence and give you time to think of the questions you might ask.

Question

Questioning is the opportunity to create huge inroads into fully understanding the sales objection, identify the real problem and allow the client to vent any built-up frustration. Start questioning by asking if you can ask questions. For example: *"Do you mind if I ask you a few questions to clarify my thinking"*? This is a polite way to show that you respect the client's concerns. Let the client speak freely and don't interrupt or anticipate an answer. This will help to release any frustration the client may have and they will then feel more receptive to listening to your answer.

Answer

After having asked questions you will be in a good position to answer and resolve the sales objection. If multiple sales objections were given, such as delivery, price and invoicing, you may need to address each objection separately.

If you are answering a price objection don't use clichés such as *"You only get what you pay for"* or *"Quality costs more"* because you will annoy the client. The answer could be:

- The small price difference between your higher quality product and your competitor's

- Comparing performance results

- Discussing potential drawbacks based on facts of the cheaper alternative

- Comparing your product with the more expensive brands or quoting additional value.

Always know why your product/service is worth its cost and keep answers brief and to the point.

Feedback

Once the client has been given the answer to their concern, ask for or confirm positive feedback to ensure they are satisfied with the answer. This respectful and caring manner will help to build the relationship. For example, *"Have I answered your concern completely?"*… *"That now satisfies the requirement, doesn't it?"* and *"I am glad we both agree."*

Move on

When the client nods their head or verbalises agreement during feedback it is time to move on to the next logical action in the sales process. This could be to write the order details or conclude the sales interview and set another appointment date.

Are sales objections good or bad? They are good because the client can express a concern, giving the salesperson the opportunity to rectify the problem or misunderstanding. They are bad if handled poorly because the sale and possibly the relationship could be at stake. Sales objections are a temporary business refusal and not to be taken personally.

To overcome sales objections, remember **AQA – FM**:

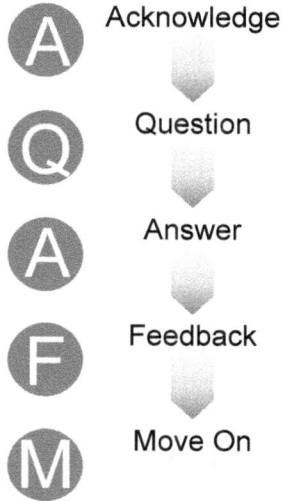

A → Acknowledge

Q → Question

A → Answer

F → Feedback

M → Move On

What Does This Chapter Mean in Your World?

1. What is your definition of a sales objection?

....

....

....

....

2. What are the common objections you hear?

....

....

....

....

3. What have you done in the past to resolve an objection? Provide an example

....

....

....

....

4. Have you been given multiple objections? If so what did you do? What was the outcome?

....

....

....

....

5. What does the acronym AQA-FM stand for?

....

....

....

....

6. What will you do to commit to doing to develop AQA-FM skills?

....

....

....

....

19

Why the old school of selling doesn't work

We have all been through the experience of buying a car

—————————— Action ——————————

There are many people out there right now who would like to replace their car with a brand new or perhaps well-kept pre-owned car. However, what stops them is the dread of going through the high pressure blatant selling tactics employed by some salespeople. If they could avoid this part of the experience they would. In fact, some people dislike the experience so much they hire professionals to buy the car for them.

My wife and I had been thinking for some time of replacing our car. It was in great condition but at 10 years old it was time to get a new vehicle. After researching extensively on the internet, we selected the type and brand of vehicle that we thought suited our needs. We headed off to a large dealership that only stocked the selected brand and had the widest selection of stock available.

Upon driving into the dealership we noticed they were in the middle of a sales weekend, complete with flags, banners, sausage sizzle and balloons. We were given a ticket and our car was parked for us. Our aim was straight forward - we would drive, validate and purchase the car that day. I was conscious not to evaluate the salesperson's selling competence and we simply wanted to confirm the safety and quality of the car and then buy.

The salesperson greeted us in a friendly manner and we expressed an interest in two models. We told him we wanted to make up our mind by selecting the one that suited us better. He didn't acknowledge our statement and proceeded to show us the first model and didn't draw a breath. He explained every detail of the vehicle, even things that we didn't care about. We followed him to the second model and he proceeded to go through all the different aspects of the two vehicles. That was fine. It didn't take long for us to decide on the one we preferred, so we then took it for a test drive. We were impressed.

We were shown an interview room and sat down to negotiate and finalise the purchase. At this point the salesperson's demeanour changed and his lack of professionalism was so obvious that I could not help but evaluating his behaviour and the selling tactics he used. I decided to go along with his charade to see where it would lead and at the same time couldn't believe what my wife and I were experiencing. If only the process of buying the car was how I had imagined it to be.

He immediately began to write our name on an order form and listed the "free" promotional items. He then asked if we would buy the car today…but we were not quoted a cost. I repeatedly asked him about the cost of the car and he kept avoided responding, other than to ask *"how much do you think it is worth?"* This became somewhat tedious so I quoted a figure that I assumed would be below their cost. He reacted quite defensively but I stuck to the quoted amount. He didn't know what to do so he left the room to confer with his sales manager. The salesperson wasn't prepared to quote a price unless we decided to buy the car that day. But how could we make a final decision if we did not know how much we would be paying? The best he could do (after multiple trips to see the sales manager) was to quote a range of numbers that fluctuated by as much as $5,000. I tried one final time to get a firm cost but was given the same run around so we told him we were not going to buy the car and ended up leaving.

This may sound like whining, or even unbelievable, but we could not believe what we had just been through. Sadly it is true and this is an incredible account of what really happened and one that had to be shared from a learning perspective. How many sales would this salesperson have lost and will continue to lose? How many perspective clients has he permanently disconnected with? Has he no idea that his behaviour is turning people away from buying?

What could this salesperson have done differently and made the sale?

- **Showed that he cared**

After the initial introduction he could have created a relaxed environment by asking if we would like to sit at his workstation so he could ask us questions about what we were after. Perhaps he could offer us a cup of tea, coffee or water, which is always a courteous gesture and a good way to begin a relationship. In this setting questions could have been asked initially about the type of car we were looking for and why, as well as ask additional questions to build rapport.

- **Asked qualifying questions**

These are specific questions relating to budget, timeframe for the decision, vehicle specifications that are not negotiable and those that are preferences. For example, a diesel engine was not negotiable but we would have accepted any one of three colour choices. Example qualifying questions he could have asked include: *"Why are you interested in this brand/model?"…"What are 2 or 3 things most important to you when buying your new car?"… "Do you have a trade-in?"… "When had you planned to buy the car? … "Do you have a budget range?"… "Do you have any colour preference?"*

- **Used structured sales language**

This is an effective way of communicating and confirming the value of the car, the most important thing from our perspective. For example, if during the questioning phase the salesperson learned that safety was a top priority then the fact the vehicle has a 5 star ANCAP Rating would be stated using structured sales language. For example: *"You mentioned that safety was very important to you. This vehicle has a 5 star ANCAP safety rating which is the highest rating so you can be assured you have a very safe vehicle."* Other areas of importance he could have said were: *"This vehicle has leather seats which not only look good but are also low maintenance"* and *"It has a diesel engine providing you with the torque you need as well as great fuel economy"*

- **Handled our objections**

Had he had answered our question about the cost of the vehicle and quoted a specific figure we would have made a decision immediately, therefore avoiding any sales objections. The objections he was given in the end were because of the frustration we felt in not getting a firm answer. It would appear that he did not have the skills to respond to our objections and perhaps to try and save the sale he could have introduced us to his sales manager.

- **Closed based on the relationship**

He could have asked a range of questions when we were test driving the vehicle to ensure it meet our core needs, therefore avoiding any surprises when it came to closing. When it did come to closing all he had to ask would be something like *"My understanding is you would prefer the metallic grey which will be available in 3 weeks. Did you want to wait the 3 weeks or would the silver one you drove be acceptable?"*

It should have been an easy sale because we were genuine buyers who liked the car. Under normal circumstances we would have closed him after the test drive by asking when we could pick up the car. Sadly his behaviour turned us off.

Applying appropriate selling skills based on the context of the relationship will more often than not create a 'pull though' sale - in other words the client closes you. Always ask qualifying questions, build rapport, and use structured sales language to make listening and communication easy for the client. If something should go astray and a sales objection is given, use AQA-FM (see Chapter 18) and always close based on the relationship and not out of date techniques founded on self-interest.

What Does This Chapter Mean in Your World?

1. Outline a buying situation when the old school of selling was used on you

....

....

....

....

2. When these old school techniques were used on you how did you feel? What was the outcome?

....

....

....

....

3. Why don't these old techniques work?

....

....

....

....

4. What qualifying questions do you ask in your field of sales?

....

....

....

....

5. Why is it important to use structured sales language based on the core needs expressed by the client?

....

....

....

....

6. How do you close based on relationship?

....

....

....

....

20

Closing the sale – why is it so misunderstood?

*Closing is an integral part of
the sales process and is used
to conclude the transaction of a sale*

_____ Action _____

Why is it that there are volumes of books, DVD's, CD's and sales seminars that focus mainly on closing the sale? It is an important step but is it the be all and end all to sales? By the sheer volume of material available and number of advertisements you would think so. The language that is used in many of these publications creates the impression that selling, and particularly closing, is adversarial. For example *"Once you have the target, agree, and then move quickly to get them to sign on the dotted line."* Target? Get them? Aren't they clients or prospective clients and don't we ask them and not get them? Some companies are so convinced that closing is a separate part of the sales process that they have dedicated sales staff referred to as "closers". At the other extreme there are salespeople who think it's beneath them to close and ask for the business. They say *"The product sells itself."*

When we have invested time and care into a client, and have found a solution to their problem, why do some salespeople avoid asking for the business? Why does this part of the sales process cause so much stress for salespeople? I once witnessed a salesperson's voice change to several octaves higher when he was about to close. Up until then the sales call was progressing harmoniously but the vocal change was so evident that the client became concerned and asked if he was okay?

When closing is treated as the most important part of the sales process an emotional divide is created between the client and salesperson that will result in a relationship problem. This is because the client senses the sale is more important than they are. They feel they are being sold to rather than them buying. Clients today are better educated and better informed than ever before and will resist robotic methods of closing. In a business to business selling environment, the client may agree to buy just to get rid of the salesperson. They will probably then phone the salesperson's company and cancel the order shortly thereafter. If the salesperson were to do a follow up call the client would avoid meeting with them. The outcome is a lost client and no future business.

The sales process does vary depending on the type of product being sold. For example, in direct selling it is common to have only one meeting to win the business. In this selling environment, many closing techniques are used and are still taught in sales courses, with a strong emphasis on building emotional involvement followed by closing…multiple times. This is because the client isn't really convinced, objects, the salesperson expects the objection and recloses. This cycle can be repeated many times. Closing terms such as the *T* or *Benjamin Franklin Close, Alternate Close, Assumptive Close* and the *Direct Close* are used.

In relationship or consultative sales however, the sales cycle is longer and more complex, involving many people both directly and indirectly in the buying process. In these selling environments, the salesperson needs to identify key problems that are causing concern. These can be high operating costs or an opportunity that may give the organisation a strategic advantage. Closing becomes easy when the right product or service is recommended; in fact, the client will initiate the close in many cases.

So, where to from here? The key to successful closing is to apply your selling skills based on a foundation of trust so the client feels comfortable and motivated to initiate the close. This makes closing a natural final step in the selling and buying process for both parties. It also sets up a precedent for future sales call interactions and sales.

Other core skills that are part of the sales process are:

1) Know your natural sales styles

Many salespeople are unaware of their dominant and back-up sales styles, and the impact of those styles on various client buying behaviours. It is common to have two or three sales styles, and with the right knowledge and skills, these can provide greater selling flexibility.

A salesperson who doesn't know their natural sales style and how to be flexible and style shift to a range of client buying behaviours will have limited success in selling to those clients who buy the way they sell or sell by pure luck in other cases. For example, building rapport with a task-oriented client is different from building rapport with a people-oriented client. Refer to Chapters 10 and 11 for more on this topic.

2) Ask the right open questions

The 20/80 rule applies when asking questions. Ask questions 20% of the time to encourage the client to respond by speaking the remaining 80% of the time. When the client talks you are in control, though they may think they are because they are doing most of the talking. A client will feel relaxed when you actively listen and share good eye contact whilst they are speaking. It shows respect and genuine caring. During the sales call this enables you to gain key information and insights into the organisation and the client as an individual.

3) Recommend/present

To effectively communicate the recommended product or service use structured sales language. The structure makes it easy for the client to understand, and allows them to make an informed decision that impacts directly on the close of the sale. The structure consists of features, transition phrases and benefits.

The transition phrase links the feature to the benefit; for example, *"What that means…"* or *"The end result will be…"* A feature is a fact about a product or service and the benefit is the value or the expected outcome for the client. The benefits that are relevant to the clients' needs will create an expression of interest or buying signal which in turn makes closing easier.

What commonly occurs without this structure is that too many features are mentioned, including those that are of little or no value to the client, while too few benefits are explained, some of which haven't been linked to what the client really needs or wants. Quite often this will result in a sales objection. As a guide, for every feature that you quote link it to a benefit by using a transition phrase. Your client will respond by giving you an expression of interest based on the benefits they are seeking and not on the features. A feature is from your company, product or service or your own perspective. Whereas a benefit is the value, how the problem will be solved, the outcome and this is what they ultimately buy.

4) Close

Closing the sale should feel natural for the client and for you. If the recommendation/presentation was implemented correctly, the client will respond with a buying signal. For example, *"If I give you the order now when could I expect delivery?"* or *"What are your terms?"* The client is interested in buying and has asked a question that has provided the opportunity to close. Simply giving an answer is not closing the sale.

Closing the sale is when the client is asked a question they can easily answer and is part of the normal flow of the conversation. So in the first example the response could be *"You can expect delivery on Friday. Would this be a suitable day or do you need it urgently?"* This answers their question and asks for a response that could lead to delivery on Friday or another day. Either one doesn't matter because as soon as the client names a date they have opened the discussion and the client is totally involved and feels in control of the decision.

If any of these core skills haven't been applied well, the client will respond with a sales objection.

Closing is an important skill to master, much like any other sales skill. It can be the easiest skill when we create the right selling environment and apply the sales process in a manner that encourages the client to initiate the close. It's only then that the client will feel that they have bought and not been sold to.

What Does This Chapter Mean in Your World?

1. What does closing the sale mean to you?

....

....

....

....

2. Have you ever had difficulty in closing a sale? If so, what were the circumstances?

....

....

....

....

3. How do you know you are quoting the right features and benefits for the client?

....

....

....

....

4. List 4 examples of features transitions and benefits

....

....

....

....

5. What is a buying signal or an expression of interest? What is its value?

....

....

....

....

6. What will you do to create a selling environment where the client feels they have bought from you rather than having been sold to?

....

....

....

....

21

Email etiquette in sales

Email like the phone has become part of our working life, yet there is a real risk of losing professional credibility when used incorrectly

_____ Action _____

Because emails leave a permanent record, this record could be an asset or a liability – for yourself and/or your company. An email can help to enhance your sales career because of the manner in which it was written, or it could make you appear to be less than what a client would expect of you.

Apply the following guidelines when using email to increase your credibility and success.

- **Use the right context**

Emails used in the right context can be an effective and efficient communication tool. Unfortunately there are situations where you can come unstuck if you use an email instead of phoning a client or seeing them in person, for example if you had to respond to a client complaint. In this situation sending an email would be totally inappropriate, with a phone call a minimum requirement and, if serious enough, a personal visit a more appropriate response.

Because clients aren't always in front of their computers, and others may only look at their emails at certain times of the day, do not send an email if you need a quick response. A phone call would be a better thing to do

- **Be polite**

'Treat others how you would like to be treated' is an old saying but it is as valid today as ever. Always be courteous in the way you write your emails, including how you greet and sign off. Be more formal with clients you do not know very well and never become complacent with those you have a good relationship with – the written form demonstrates the respect you have for them. Use words when greeting a client with *"Dear…"* and a well-established client with *"Hi…"* and use phrases and words such as *"Thank you"*… *"Please"*… *"I appreciate your help"* and *"Best regards"*

- **Be concise**

Emails are a fast medium that requires a different style of writing. Do not send long-winded emails that could be tedious to read and at best may be only partially read or comprehended. To minimise this from happening, use short paragraphs and a line gap between each paragraph to make reading email visually comfortable. Keep sentences to a maximum of 20 words. Ideally aim to keep your email messages to one subject per email, thus avoiding potential confusion.

- **Use correct spelling, grammar and punctuation**

If you don't do so already, develop the habit of reading your emails twice before sending. This will allow you to find any errors. Spelling mistakes, incorrect or poor grammar, and the use of slang could impact on your creditability and that of your company's. Punctuation has become minimalist as email communication has evolved. So overuse may communicate that you are old fashioned and missing punctuation where it should be risk losing your intended meaning.

- **Use sentence case**

Capitalise the first letter of a word but don't use CAPITAL LETTERS throughout your email. It is the equivalent of verbally shouting and may even be interpreted as a verbal attack. At the other end of the spectrum, using all lower case letters can be perceived that the sender is subservient or lacks education. For example, "what if i were to meet with you on thursday instead of monday?" This should be "What if I were to meet with you on Thursday instead of Monday?" If you need to emphasise a key word use bold formatting.

- **Replace abbreviations and emoticons**

Abbreviations and emoticons have become popular to save time and keystrokes but these do imply tone of voice and problems can occur when someone is unfamiliar with this form of communication. For example, use of the abbreviation FWIW (For What It's Worth) and the emoticon :-). These forms of communication might be suitable with family and friends but are generally not appropriate for business use. Acronyms may be popular within your industry but confusion may occur if the client is new to the industry and does not know their meaning. To avoid these and other difficulties, such as unusual fonts or font sizes, type complete sentences and use standard fonts such as Arial and legible size fonts, perhaps 11 or 12.

- **Use active language**

The active verb should be used wherever possible because it is a direct and more personal way of communicating. For example *"I will process your order immediately"* versus a passive form which is *"Your order will be processed immediately."* Active language also communicates confidence and personal responsibility.

- **Effective message response times**

All emails should ideally be replied to within the same business day or at a time requested by the client. If this is not possible, call the client and let them know when you will answer their email or ask a colleague to do it for you. In a situation where the client has asked a series of questions that require answers and you believe there would, in all probability, be additional questions that require an answer, then go a step further and pre-empt those missed questions and provide answers.

- **Using Cc, Bcc and Return Receipt**

Cc, (carbon copy) *Bcc*, (blind carbon copy) *Reply* and *Reply All* should only be sent to those who are immediately involved in the email communication. Bcc is used when you have a large list of people you need to email and not everyone on the list needs to know who is on it. Continue with email threads as long as the subject relates to the original subject matter, so previous emails can be referred to if necessary. When replying to an email that has multiple recipients, delete those addresses that your response doesn't apply to. Use Return Receipt sparingly because unless it's really necessary it can be annoying

- **Subject line**

The subject line should always be directly linked to the content, for example if you have been given a referral put that person's name as the subject line. *"Rachael Sanders ask me to contact you."*

- **Using email forwarding and attachments**

Never open an attachment from a person you don't know. If you have multiple attachments and want to prevent an email from bouncing because of the size of the files then send them over several emails. Alternatively, compress large files before sending and/or use one of the many services available that handle large files like Memeo Send or Drop Box.

Use PDFs wherever possible and make sure the recipient has software that can open your attachment. When forwarding an email remove any irrelevant information such as previous email addresses, headers and comments from other forwarders

- **Using confidential information privacy**

Email is deemed to be owned by the company and can be salvaged and scrutinised in a court of law. Sending emails that contain libellous, racist, slanderous or offensive remarks can be subject to litigation. Political, sexual, or religious humour emails could put your credibility into question because the recipient may not share your views. Be careful what you forward because you could also be infringing copyright law. Treat email as being not secure and don't send anything that you wouldn't send to your mother

- **Using disclaimers to emails**

Disclaimers should be added to all internal and external emails to help protect the company from liability.

Email is a great communication tool that can add to your sales credibility when used in the right context and with content that is written in a professional manner.

What Does This Chapter Mean in Your World?

1. Describe a situation when you wrote an email that was embarrassing. What happened?

....

....

....

....

2. Name 5 of the email guidelines

....

....

....

....

3. Of the 13 guidelines which ones do you believe you don't use or could use better?

....

....

....

....

4. Explain what is meant by using active language in emails and provide 2 examples

....

....

....

....

5. When would you use Bcc instead of Cc?

....

....

....

....

6. What has been the most valuable lesson you learnt in this chapter and will commit to implementing?

....

....

....

....

References

Ken Keis with Everett T. Robinson, 2011, **Why Aren't You More Like Me**: second edition, Friesens Corporation, Altona MB Canada

Terry D. Anderson, Ph.D., Ken Keis, MBA., and Bruce Wares, 2008, Sales Style Indicator, Consulting Resource Group International, Inc

I have had an association with The Consulting Resource Group since 1994. Chapters 9 and 10 draw on The Sales Style Indicator one of the self-assessment tools developed by this company. The integrity of the company and its products and services are of the highest standard. The website is www.crgleader.com

George W. Dudley and Shannon L. Goodson, 2007, **The Psychology of Sales Call Reluctance**, Behavioural Sciences Research Press Inc.

The percentage figures quoted in Chapter 8 are from this publication. The book diagnoses the emotional causes of sales call reluctance and how to identify their symptoms. The authors provide the solutions to the various call reluctance problems. The book is backed by solid research in the behavioural sciences and real world testing with salespeople.

Ron Willingham, 2006, The Inner Game of Selling, Free Press

Stephen R. Covey, 1994, **The 7 Habits of Highly Effective People**, McPherson's Printing Group Australia

The references made in the Foreword by Paul Sparks are from this exceptionally insightful book on human behaviour and should be part of everyone's library. Though it was first published in 1989 it is a timeless self-development book. In August 2011 Time listed the book as one of 'The 25 Most Influential Business Management Books'.

Wikipedia has been used whenever a definition is quoted. Wikipedia is an encyclopaedia written collaboratively by the people who use it.